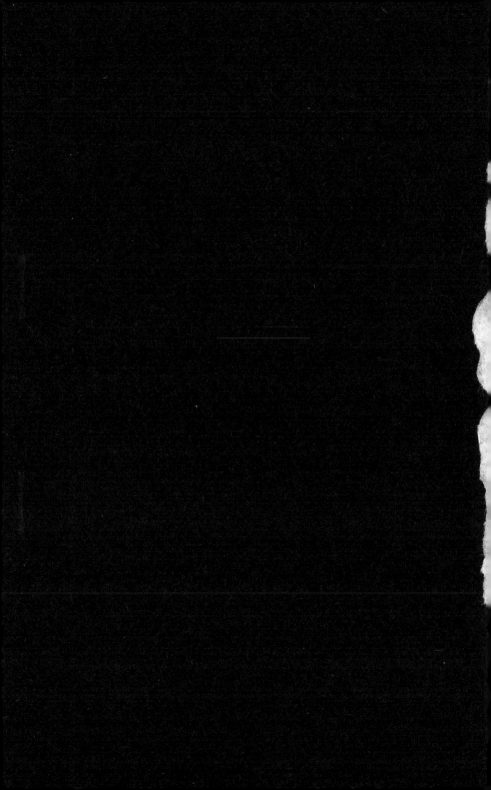

RICHARD A. ISAY

BEING HOMOSEXUAL

GAY MEN AND THEIR DEVELOPMENT

JASON ARONSON INC.
Northvale, New Jersey
London

The lines from "Esthétique du mal" are reprinted from *The Collected Poems of Wallace Stevens,* © 1947 by Wallace Stevens. Reprinted by permission of Alfred A. Knopf.

Chapters 1, 2, 3, 4 and 8 are adapted from the following articles written by Richard A. Isay, which appeared in *The Psychoanalytic Study of the Child,* published by Yale University Press: "On the Analytic Therapy of Homosexual Men" in Volume 40, © 1985 by Albert J. Solnit, Ruth S. Eissler and Peter B. Neubauer, "The Development of Sexual Identity in Homosexual Men" in Volume 41, © 1986 by Albert J. Solnit and Peter B. Neubauer, "Fathers and Their Homosexually Inclined Sons in Childhood" in Volume 42, © 1987 by Albert J. Solnit and Peter B. Neubauer. Reprinted by permission of Yale University Press.

Chapter 7 is adapted from Chapter 13 of *The Psychology of Men: New Psychoanalytic Perspectives,* edited by Gerald I. Fogel, Frederick M. Lane and Robert S. Liebert. Copyright © 1986 by Basic Books, Inc., Publishers. Reprinted by permission of Basic Books, Inc., Publishers.

THE MASTER WORK SERIES
Softcover edition 1994

Library of Congress Cataloging-in-Publication Data

ISBN: 1-56821-276-3
Library of Congress Catalog Card Number: 94-71089

Manufactured in the United States of America. Jason Aronson Inc. offers books and cassettes. For information and catalog write to Jason Aronson Inc., 230 Livingston Street, Northvale, New Jersey 07647.

For Gordon Harrell

ACKNOWLEDGMENTS

Chapters 1, 2, 3, 4, and 8 of this book evolved from articles I have written over the past several years. "On the Analytic Therapy of Homosexual Men," "The Development of Sexual Identity in Homosexual Men," and "Fathers and Their Homosexually Inclined Sons in Childhood" were originally published in Volumes 40, 41, and 42 of *The Psychoanalytic Study of the Child* (New Haven: Yale University Press). Portions of these articles are included here in a different form, with the permission of the publisher. I am grateful to Albert Solnit and Peter Neubauer, the managing editors of these volumes, for initially publishing these papers. Portions of Chapter 7, based on the chapter "Homosexuality in Homosexual and Heterosexual Men: Some Distinctions and Implications for Treatment," in Gerald Fogel, Frederick Lane, and Robert Liebert, eds., *The Psychology of Men* (New York: Basic Books, 1986), are reprinted here with the publisher's permission.

Papers on which portions of this book are based have also been presented and discussed at meetings of the American Psychoanalytic Association, the Association for Psychoanalytic Medicine (New York), Boston Psychoanalytic Society and Institute, Canadian Psychoanalytic Society (Quebec English Branch), Chicago Psychoanalytic Society, North Carolina Psychoanalytic Society, Philadelphia Psychoanalytic Society, Psychoanalytic Association of New York, Pittsburgh Psychoanalytic Society, Washington Psychoanalytic Society, and the Western New England Psychoanalytic Society. I have also had the opportunity to discuss some of my ideas at Grand Rounds in the Departments of Psychiatry at the Allen Memorial Institute (Montreal), Cornell University Medical Center, North Shore University Hospital, Ottawa General Hospital, Roosevelt Hospital, St. Luke's Hospital, the University of California (San Francisco), and as the First Annual Lecturer at the San Francisco Postgraduate Institute of Psychoanalytic Psychotherapy on March 29, 1986.

I am also grateful for the opportunities I have had to discuss parts of this book at annual meetings of the American Psychiatric Association in 1986, 1987, and 1988 on symposia organized and chaired by my friend and colleague Robert Cabaj; at a symposium on "Homosexuality/Heterosexuality" sponsored by the Kinsey Institute for Research (May 22–25, 1986); at scientific meetings of the Gay Psychiatrists of New York (June 1986 and 1987); at a psychotherapy symposium sponsored by the Cambridge Hospital (June 4, 1988); and at the Second International Conference on Gay and Lesbian Health (July 1988).

Gordon Harrell has been indirectly responsible for many of the ideas and attitudes expressed in the book, and for much more as well. I am very grateful for everything he has given me.

Others to whom I wish to express special thanks are David Arndt, Donald Cohen, Stephen Goldfinger, Richard Friedman, Douglas Heath, Gilbert Herdt, Jane Isay, Robert Kertzner, David Kessler, Larry Kramer, Stanley Leavy, David McWhirter, Myron Markel, Judd Marmor, George Pollock, Arnold Rothstein, Frank Rundle, Winfield Scott, and Stephen Weissman.

My editor, Linda Healey, has been enthusiastic about this project from the start. I am grateful for that, as well as for her competence. Andrea Miller, who typed and corrected many drafts of the manuscript, has been a pleasure to work with.

Finally, it has been my patients, through their willingness to share with me their most private fears, pleasures, thoughts, and feelings, who made this book possible.

R.A.I.

CONTENTS

Introduction   3

1   What Is Homosexuality?   11

2   Childhood and Early Homosexual Identity   23

3   Fathers and Their Homosexual Sons in Childhood   32

4   Adolescence and Young Adulthood of Gay Men   47

5   AIDS: The Development of Healthy Gay Men
     and Homophobia   67

6   Lovers and Others: Gay Relationships   82

7   The Homoerotic Fantasy of Heterosexual Men
     and the Question of Bisexuality   94

8   Psychotherapy with Gay Men   109

9   Society and Gay Men   128

Notes   135

Index   151

The greatest poverty is not to live
In a physical world, to feel that one's desire
Is too difficult to tell from despair.

—WALLACE STEVENS, *Esthétique du mal*

BEING HOMOSEXUAL

GAY MEN
AND THEIR
DEVELOPMENT

Introduction

IN 1935, in his compassionate "Letter to an American Mother" whose son was homosexual, Freud wrote:

> Homosexuality is assuredly no advantage, but it is nothing to be ashamed of, no vice, no degradation, it cannot be classified as an illness. . . . Many highly respectable individuals of ancient and modern times have been homosexuals, several of the greatest men among them (Plato, Michelangelo, Leonardo da Vinci, etc.). It is a great injustice to persecute homosexuality as a crime, and cruelty too.[1]

Although Freud equivocated about whether or not homosexuality was in itself pathological, unlike contemporary psychoanalysts he did not consider homosexuals as "sick." In a 1905 interview published in the newspaper *Die Zeit* he stated:

> I am . . . of the firm conviction that homosexuals must not be treated as sick people. . . . Wouldn't that oblige us to characterize as sick many great thinkers and scholars . . . whom we admire precisely because of their mental health? Homosexual persons are not sick. They also do not belong in a court of law![2]

3

Sixty years later two American psychoanalysts, concerned about the increasingly aggressive attempts of homosexuals to achieve civil rights, were quoted in *The New York Times*. Irving Bieber, who had directed an extensive study of homosexual men,[3] stated that "he does not approve the attempt by organized homosexuals to promote the idea that they represent just another minority, since their minority status is based on illness. . . ." The second analyst, Charles Socarides, who still writes extensively about homosexuals, is quoted as saying: "The homosexual is ill, and anything that tends to hide that fact reduces his chances of seeking and obtaining treatment. . . . If they were to achieve social acceptance it would increase this difficulty."[4] These analysts were expressing a conviction that continues to shape the thinking and practice of the American psychoanalytic community.

Traditional psychoanalytic theory asserts that unimpeded normal development leads to the mature expression of heterosexuality. Homosexuality, the theory holds, is caused by severe early developmental disturbances. These early disruptions are said to produce the conflict that results both in a turning away from heterosexuality and in the severe personality disorders that all homosexuals are believed to suffer.

My work with more than forty gay men either in a classical analysis or in analytically oriented therapy over the past twenty years, along with personal observation, has led me to conclude that the expression of their sexuality is both normal and growth-enhancing for gay men. My clinical work and the empirical studies done by others also suggest that, like heterosexuality, homosexuality is constitutional in origin.

Many who read this will believe that, even if I am correct that homosexuality is constitutional, disease and malformation may also be inborn, and that, similarly, homosexuality is a defect. But the analogy derives from social prejudice which, in this instance, causes social values to be confused with health values.

Some analysts regard gay men as abnormal because they act out sexual impulses that are not socially acceptable, rather than sublimating their sexuality for the sake of social adaptation. When psychoanalysts speak of their patients "acting out," they are usually referring to the expression of fantasies or impulses that, rather than being articulated in the analytic session, are being acted on. Those who consistently "act out" their impulses are traditionally regarded as not being good analysands.[5] Although it is considered valuable for patients and nonpatients alike to be able to recognize and tolerate a wide range of aggressive and sexual impulses and fantasies, the emphasis in traditional psychoanalysis is on the containment of these impulses in order to conform to society's demands and expectations. This, to paraphrase Freud, is the price one pays for being civilized.[6]

In theory, psychoanalysts do not feel that adaptation should take place at the expense of one's internal world. However, when it comes to patients acting and being in the world, most dynamically oriented psychotherapists tend to be governed in their clinical work by the conviction that what is healthy is what is socially adaptive.

Reinforcing the tendency to encourage socially adaptive behavior in homosexual patients is the orthodox psychoanalytic position that homosexuals are abnormal because they are not heterosexual. I believe this position expresses the social bias of the society in which psychoanalysts live and work. It is a theory that has interfered with our being able to conceptualize a developmental pathway for gay men and thus has seriously impeded our capacity to provide a psychotherapy that is neutral and unbiased by cultural expectations.[7]

My views are a return to Freud, who, while describing a

variety of environmental or "accidental" causes of homosexuality, never lost sight of the major importance of biological factors in understanding the variety of sexual manifestations in human beings. "It may be questioned," he wrote, "whether the various accidental influences would be sufficient to explain the acquisition of [homosexuality] without the cooperation of something in the subject himself."[8]

And on the question of whether homosexuals can be good analysts, Freud, responding to an inquiry from Ernest Jones about accepting homosexuals for psychoanalytic training, wrote: "We do not on principle want to exclude such persons because we also cannot condone their legal persecution. We believe that a decision in such cases should be reserved for an examination of the individual's other qualities."[9] However, organized psychoanalysis today still generally excludes homosexuals from training, because of the conviction that all gay men suffer from such early and severe developmental defects that they cannot be good analysts.

From its inception as a radical movement, psychoanalysis has become a conservative one, and with regard to the issue of homosexuals and homosexuality, is far to the right of all other mental-health professions. How has this bias evolved— a bias that, while by no means exclusively American, appears to be most firmly rooted in the American psychoanalytic tradition?

During World War II many American analysts held important positions in military psychiatry, and on their return from the service became chairmen of or influential in Departments of Psychiatry in the United States. After the war they consolidated the gains they had made in achieving a significant degree of respectability for the new science of psychoanalysis by further strengthening its ties to psychiatry, medicine, and the disease model. Their efforts served to gain legitimacy for psychoanalysis as a mental-health profession and economic benefit for its members.

Shortly before the outbreak of World War II, there was an influx of European analysts fleeing Nazi persecution. Many of these refugees, understandably preoccupied with being accepted in a new homeland and insecure about their financial and professional futures, were not eager to pose challenges to established social and professional organizations. Some who in Europe had been outspoken critics of bourgeois culture felt particularly threatened at the outset of the cold war and during the McCarthy era in the forties and early fifties and were wary of pursuing their radical intellectual and social interests.[10] These European analysts, aligned with others who were eager for organized psychoanalysis to tie itself to medicine, committed American psychoanalysis to orthodoxy and social conformity.[11] During this time, when there were purges of homosexuals from government, there was also consolidation within psychoanalysis of the theory of the pathological adaptation of homosexuals, and the exclusion of homosexuals from analytic institutes became customary.[12]

A clinical theory has naturally evolved from the supposition that homosexuality results from early developmental disturbance. This theory, which guides the work of most traditional analytic therapists, holds that homosexuals can and should be heterosexual if their full potential is to be realized and they are to live lives as productive and free of internal conflict as possible.[13]

When the idea that it is possible and desirable to change a homosexual into a heterosexual is applied clinically, it may cause a variety of severe symptoms, particularly depression and anxiety, as a result of the undermining of self-esteem (see Chapter 8). It has led some gay men to attempt to behave heterosexually in order to conform to their analyst's explicitly stated or implicit expectations. These efforts are psychologically harmful if a gay man cannot gain pleasure from his sexual activity, for the failure to do so adds to his perception that he is impaired because of his sexual orientation. The practitioner's perceived need for his homosexual patient to be heterosexual has also resulted in many unhappy marriages, with serious social and psychological consequences for all family members.

The current basic conviction of most analytically oriented therapists that homosexuality is pathological has driven most gay men to look for psychological assistance from other than orthodox psychoanalysts. Given all of the above, the decision of gay men to seek help elsewhere is, I believe, wise. On the other hand, there are many aspects of psychoanalytic theory that, when appropriately applied, are useful in understanding human behavior and helpful in relieving emotional pain. The clinical theory, which holds to the centrality of unconscious conflict in causing psychological pain and to the importance of childhood experiences in shaping adult character, is helpful in understanding the suffering of many persons. Likewise, analytic technique which aims to lift defenses against unconscious feelings and memories and attends to the reliving of old conflicts in the transference is of enormous help to many patients. I believe, however, that the proper application of psychoanalytic technique to the treatment of homosexuals demands that his sexuality, like the heterosexuality of a straight man, be perceived as normal for him.

Throughout this book, I use the concepts of health and normality interchangeably. By these terms I am referring to the gay man's potential for a well-integrated personality, a personality in which there is reasonable intrapsychic harmony, so that he may feel positive about his personal identity as a homosexual and may work and live without significant hindrance from intrapsychic conflict. I draw on a concept of health that emphasizes the individual's capacity for self-esteem and a positive self-image, traits that make it possible for all persons to respect and love others and to be nourished by the respect and love of others.

In order to move from the medical and pathological perspective of homosexuality that I do not find either valid or clinically useful, I use the words "gay" and "homosexual" synonymously. I do not intend "gay" to have any political connotation, and I do not reserve the term for those men who are involved in a gay community or a gay life-style, or are necessarily self-identified as "gay."[14]

My observations and inferences about the normal development of gay men are based largely on data gathered during the course of analyses or intensive psychotherapy of my patients. This has afforded me an unusual opportunity to hear in detail about the early lives, development, and current lifestyles, as well as the conflicts, of a large number of gay men, many of whom are well-functioning mental-health professionals. Although this is not a random sample of gay men, I believe these men are distinguished from any nonpatient population more by their psychological curiosity and by their determination and motivation to live lives as free of conflict as possible than by any greater degree of neurotic difficulty.

My patients consist largely of gay men who are generally accepting of their sexuality. No one has come to me specifically for help in changing his sexual orientation. A man who is dissatisfied with himself as a gay man would seek out an analyst who held to the prevailing views of homosexuality. And it is from the treatment of gay men who are in severe conflict about their sexuality that analysts have traditionally gathered their observations and drawn conclusions. But severe conflict over sexual identity and a wish to be heterosexual are not representative of the general gay population; they are symptomatic of more disturbed gay men.[15]

Of course, my observations are subject to the normal distortions of any person's perceptions, and my conclusions, in spite of my best efforts to be objective, are subject to distortions caused by my own interpretation of what I am hearing. I do not consider my observations necessarily correct in all regards. I do consider them a framework for an understanding of the normal development of gay men.

From these efforts has evolved a therapy based on psychodynamic principles which is not biased by the notion that all homosexuals are latent heterosexuals who are deviant or perverted in their sexuality because of emotional trauma. In Chapter 8 I discuss some of the treatment issues for gay men seeking help and for the therapists giving help. I hope that this book enables clinicians who work with gay men to do so more effectively and with greater empathy and understanding.

This book is also intended for gay men. I hope it provides them with a richer understanding of their own development.

1

What Is Homosexuality?

Those who are halves of a male whole pursue males, and being slices, so to speak, of the male, love men throughout their boyhood, and take pleasure in physical contact with men. Such boys and lads are the best of their generation, because they are the most manly.

—PLATO, *The Symposium*

HOMOSEXUAL MEN have a predominant erotic attraction to others of the same sex. Their sexual fantasies are either entirely or almost entirely directed toward other men, and have been so since childhood. Because sexual behavior may be inhibited by societal pressure or by internal conflict, a man need not engage in sexual activity to be homosexual. Those who have homosexual contacts but, because of censorious social pressures, intrapsychic conflict, or both, are unable to accept that they are gay are also homosexual. There are others who may not even have conscious access to their homoerotic fantasies because they repress, suppress, or deny them. Their fantasies become more available to them during a properly conducted analysis or therapy, and I also consider them to be homosexual.[1]

The seven-point scale (0–6) of Alfred Kinsey and his associates emphasizes the behavior and conscious sexual interest of their respondents.[2] 5's and 6's on Kinsey's scale indicate those with exclusive or nearly exclusive homoerotic behavior. I have found sexual fantasy to be a more clinically useful way of defining homosexuality than behavior. Just as a man would be considered heterosexual even if he was constrained from expressing or elected not to express his sexuality for reasons of age, circumstance, or vocation, I am taking into account that some gay men may not express their homoerotic impulses because of internal conflict, social bias, or personal choice.

Systematic investigations by psychologists over the years suggest that there is no greater psychopathology in gay men than in heterosexuals. The best-known of these are Evelyn Hooker's studies, designed to determine the usefulness of projective psychological tests in diagnosing overt homosexual behavior and to assess whether there are distinctive personality characteristics in exclusively homosexual men.[3] No distinguishing psychopathology or greater degree of social or psychological maladjustment was found in homosexual men. A number of other investigators, using both projective tests to elicit unconscious conflict and objective psychological tests to draw out more conscious, recognized difficulties, have been unable to find greater pathology among homosexuals than among heterosexuals.[4]

The distinguished studies by Kinsey and associates that verified a high incidence of homosexual behavior would tend to support the perspective that homosexuality is a nonpathological variant of human sexuality. They surveyed approximately five thousand white American males and found that 4 percent of the adult white male population are exclusively homosexual throughout their lives after adolescence, and that about 10 percent of the total male population are exclusively homosexual for at least three years sometime between the ages of sixteen and sixty-five. A number of European surveys report a comparably high incidence of homosexuality and homosexual experiences.[5]

Clellan Ford and Frank Beach in their cross-cultural investigations and studies of subhuman primates support the observation that regarding homosexuality as pathological is an expression of cultural bias. In the majority of the seventy-six societies they studied, homosexual activities were considered either socially acceptable or normal:

> Some homosexual behavior occurs in a great many human societies. It tends to be more common in adolescence than in adulthood and appears to be practiced more frequently by men than women. This is also true of the other animal species . . . and particularly so in the infrahuman primates. Even in societies which severely restrict homosexual tendencies, however, some individuals do exhibit homosexual behavior. . . . Within the societies which, unlike our own, provide socially acceptable homosexual roles, a number of individuals, predominantly men, choose to exhibit some measure of homosexual behavior.[6]

Of course, in Western societies influenced by the Judeo-Christian view of sexuality and morality, homosexuality has been barely tolerated, and in many countries it has been outlawed. Until the late fifties, Great Britain had imposed severe legal penalties against homosexuals. The Wolfenden Committee was appointed by the House of Lords in 1954 to study these laws. Their report supported the decriminalization in England of homosexual acts between consenting adults in private and was strongly critical of the belief that homosexuality is a disease. The committee pointed out that when there are no symptoms associated with a behavior that may be compatible with "full mental health," then that behavior cannot be regarded as a disease.[7]

In careful consideration of such studies, and because of the recommendations of prominent psychiatrists such as Judd Marmor, who is also an analyst, along with the effective testimony of gays on the social stigmatization of labeling homosexuality a disease, the American Psychiatric Association in 1973 decided to remove homosexuality from its official *Diagnostic and Statistic Manual of Mental Disorders*.[8] Psychoanalysis, in contrast to and in spite of such evidence, remains committed to the conviction that homosexuality is always pathological. Homosexuality is seen ipso facto as a perverse and deviant form of sexuality because gay men do not reach the theoretical "normal" developmental end point of resolving the Oedipal conflict by desiring someone like their mothers through an identification with their fathers.

Psychoanalysts have looked at the early-childhood histories of gay men they have seen as patients, and isolated what appear to be environmental determinants of their desire for other men rather than for women as lovers. Some have said that predilection for a same-sex love object is caused by a close-binding, hostile mother who undermines her son's masculinity by blocking the development of independence, interfering with the father-son relationship, and inducing a fear of women.[9] Others emphasize the role of an absent, weak, detached, or hostile father who makes it impossible for the child to separate from his dominating mother.[10]

These psychodynamic conceptions can be traced to Freud, who at one time or other implicated a number of environmental factors in the origin of homosexuality. His major interest, however, was in developing the clinical technique of psychoanalysis. He felt an obligation to stress those environmental factors which psychoanalysts could investigate, rather than emphasize the role of those constitutional factors that he always believed to be of major importance in the formation of a homosexual orientation. [11]

After Freud's death, psychoanalysts became intent upon removing the ambiguity in his ideas about the nature and origin of homosexuality, and decisively settled on a pathological model. The first to criticize Freud's theory was Sandor Rado, who considered the idea of genetically predisposed bisexuality to be biologically unsound, of no clinical value, and of little use in guiding future research. [12] He believed that Freud's concept of an inborn potential for homosexuality led analysts to lower unnecessarily their therapeutic expectations when it came to treating homosexual patients. He believed homosexuality to be the phobic response of a man who is so incapacitated by anxiety evoked by his mother, and subsequently by fears of all women, that he applies "aberrant forms of stimulation to his standard genital equipment." [13] Other psychoanalysts such as Irving Bieber, Lionel Ovesey, and Charles Socarides were influenced by Rado and elaborated on this theory of anxiety caused by an intense attachment to the mother. They consider homosexuality to be profoundly pathological, and all homosexuals to be seriously disturbed.

My clinical work with gay men for more than twenty years has brought me to the conviction that homosexuality is a nonpathological variant of human sexuality. Unlike most other psychoanalysts, I have found no greater psychopathology in my gay patients than in my heterosexual patients. But also, unlike other psychoanalysts, I work with gay men who generally accept their sexuality. The early aberrant relations with mothers described by most analysts appear to be more characteristic of men who are dissatisfied with their sexuality than of gay men in general. [14]

Two men discussed later in this book, Benjamin and Carl, had severe character disturbances of a narcissistic and masochistic nature. Of all my patients, they had the most difficulty accepting themselves as gay men. They also had more difficulty than others with intimacy, and both had a need for random sexual encounters, which is not characteristic of all gay men. They were the only men whose mothers seemed to bind their sons to them because of their own needs and could not permit adequate separation and self-differentiation to occur. If these men had been heterosexual, they would have had similarly poor self-images, identity diffusion, masochistic, self-punitive tendencies, and difficulties with intimate relationships due to early injury to their self-esteem.

Some who have studied homosexuality emphasize the importance of personal choice in its development. For example, there are women who, out of feminist conviction, sexually bonded with other women for purposes of power in our male-dominated society but later became disenchanted with the women's movement, and chose to leave their partners to seek more traditional lives and roles. Political and social motives for determining the sexual object are significantly less frequent in the sexual bonding of gay men, in part, perhaps, because the price paid in social discrimination is probably higher for gay men living together than it is for gay women. More important, there is no evidence to suggest that gay men can revert to heterosexual behavior without great difficulty and without becoming anxious or depressed. Therefore, if choice plays a role in influencing the sexuality of some women, it may be because anatomical differences make it easier for women to perform with either sex, more women are bisexual, or forms of intimacy that are not sexual may be more important for women than for men. I have never encountered in my practice a gay man who "chooses" to be homosexual, but it is also true that most gay men I know prefer their sexuality to heterosexuality, since what is experienced as normal and natural is usually preferred, even if such behavior is socially disadvantageous.

Although homosexuality in men is more appropriately labeled an "orientation" than a "choice" or a "preference," many homosexual men do prefer the lives they lead to the more conventional lives of most heterosexuals. While some may mourn the fact that they do not have children or the comfort and security offered by a traditional family, there are also many gay men who, like some single heterosexuals, do not want a traditional family structure and enjoy the economic benefits and relative independence of not having a family.

Some sociobiologists have proposed that homosexuality may have an evolutionary basis. Proceeding from the idea that traits survive that are adaptive, they suggest that the personal and economic advantages that accrue to the relatives of gay men may contribute to fostering the survival of genes for homosexuality. These benefits could offset any genetic disadvantage that occurs because fewer homosexuals than heterosexuals have children.[15] E. O. Wilson has suggested that homosexuality may be a "normal" trait "that evolved as an important element of early human social organization. Homosexuals may be the genetic carriers of some of mankind's rare altruistic impulses."[16] At present there is no empirical support for the idea of kin selection as a way of passing on a gene for homosexuality. It is questionable as well whether homosexuals have any privileged status in our society, and, if some do, to what extent the benefits of such privilege are shared by their relatives.[17]

All psychoanalytic theories of homosexuality suggest that homosexual men suffer from a deficiency in their masculinity. Either a distant father fails to help his son separate from his mother, or the mother pathologically binds the boy to her, sometimes because of her own ungratified needs to be mothered. She attempts to get what she lacks by giving, but does so with enormous rage that is emotionally draining to her and wounding to the child. In both scenarios, gay men are believed to have either a conscious or an unconscious feeling of femininity. To put it simply, traditional analysts believe a man cannot be homosexual without also being and/or feeling effeminate.

Extensive identification with the mother may occur during the first two or three years in the development of any child whose mother fails to let him separate from her because of her neurotic needs or where a father is unable or unwilling to assist the child in disidentifying during this stage of union and merger with the mother.[18] This early identification may sometimes result in profound disturbance in a sense of one's masculinity. However, mothers or fathers who inhibit the development of their sons in this way are by no means restricted to gay men only; I do not believe that such early difficulties in separation occur significantly more often in gay men than in heterosexuals. None of my patients had any confusion or concern about the sex to which he belonged.

Richard Green studied forty-four boys who were "feminine" and found that two-thirds became homosexual or bisexual adults.[19] His findings confirmed earlier studies that indicated the prevalence of homosexuality in adults who as children had displayed "effeminate" behavior, avoided rough-and-tumble aggressive play, and were generally unassertive.[20] One should not conclude from these studies, however, that most gay men are "feminine" in childhood or that the origin of homosexuality is linked to a lack of masculinity.

Some investigators have stressed the importance of neuroendocrine factors in the development of homosexuality. One has hypothesized, on the basis of his studies, that a relative deficit prenatally of the male hormone, androgen, leads to homosexuality by causing a "predominantly female differentiated brain."[21] The evidence regarding the importance of prenatal endocrine influence on the development of a homosexual object choice is contradictory, and the methodological errors in some of the research has cast doubt on its reliability.[22] Richard Friedman has suggested that one may see the childhood aversion to aggressive play as evidence of the prenatal endocrine influence on sexual orientation.[23]

On the basis of my clinical work, I have come to believe that at ages three, four, five, and six some homosexual children assume opposite gender characteristics in order to attract and sustain the attention of the father (see Chapter 3). These are usually such attributes as sensitivity, gentleness, and a lack of interest in aggressive sports. Some homosexual children may also seem noticeably feminine in manner, dress, and behavior. I believe that they develop these characteristics for the same reason that heterosexual boys may adopt certain of their fathers' attributes, in order to attract, first, the mother's interest and, later, someone like the mother. These identifications in homosexual children appear to follow the manifestation of the sexual orientation and the erotic attachment to the father and not to precede them.[24]

Some homosexual boys have difficulty experiencing themselves as masculine because they have same-sex fantasies and attractions. In our society, where there is such a rigid delineation of what is masculine and what is feminine, they can see themselves only as the "other," as feminine. Because, in our society, there is a need to have gender behavior conform to anatomy, many gay men, through deliberate effort during preadolescence (ages ten, eleven, and twelve) and adolescence, lose many of the "feminine"-like qualities they might have acquired from identification with the mother or a mother surrogate in earlier childhood.

It is important to keep in mind that the exaggerated feminine behavior, or "camp," that some adult gay men enjoy is not causally linked to the development of their sexual orientation. Such behavior contains varying degrees of conscious self-mockery designed to flaunt conventional gender labeling. In our society a gay man is labeled "feminine" simply because he desires or loves other men. It is the angry recognition and flaunting of this conventional cultural stereotype that to a large extent accounts for "camp" behavior, rather than a disturbance in gender identity.

Since I have found no distinction between the parenting of my gay patients and the parenting of my heterosexual patients, I believe it is the constitutional presence of homosexuality, rather than the environment, that accounts for sexual orientation. There may, of course, be a hierarchy of environmental factors that more or less readily permits a predisposition to homosexuality to manifest itself. However, my clinical experience suggests that while the early environment has considerable influence on the manner in which sexuality is expressed, it has an indiscernible influence on the sex of the love object.

There is some empirical evidence that there is a biological basis for homosexuality, as is generally assumed to be the case for heterosexuality. A recent study found a difference in nuclei in the anterior hypothalamus between heterosexual men and homosexual men who had died of AIDS.[25] Although the study needs to be replicated with a diverse sample of healthy gay men, it does suggest a biological basis for male homosexuality.

One investigation found a concordance for homosexual behavior only slightly higher than normal in dizygotic twins, but one hundred percent in monozygotic twins.[26] A more recent study showed that the proportion of homosexuals was significantly greater in monozygotic twins than for either dizygotic twins or adoptive brothers.[27] And research published in 1993 demonstrated a location on the X chromosome that correlates with being homosexual in families in which there are two gay brothers.[28] These findings strongly suggest that homosexuality in men is both constitutional and heritable.

An emphasis on hereditary factors, which takes into account this data from family and twin studies, makes it more understandable that homosexual and heterosexual men may have identical or similar family environments. The possibility that heredity might influence prenatal neuroendocrine factors cannot be excluded, even though the evidence is inconclusive. The genetic hypothesis is also compatible with theories that suggest there is an evolutionary trend toward greater flexibility and diversity in human sexuality.[29]

From a clinical standpoint, it is helpful to view sexual orientation as constitutional. Since efforts to change homosexual behavior to heterosexual are injurious to the self-esteem of the gay man, and efforts to change core sexuality appear to be futile, perceiving sexuality as constitutional permits the therapist to understand and investigate the expression of a homosexual orientation with the same neutrality as he does heterosexuality (see Chapter 8).

While I regard sexual orientation itself as immutable from birth, the manner in which it is expressed appears to have multiple and diverse roots that may be profoundly influenced by a variety of early experiences. A boy who grows up with a dominant mother who uses him to fulfill ungratified needs of her own will have the same chance of becoming gay as he would if he were raised by a mother who ideally nurtures his growth and development. However, it is likely that this child as an adult, whether gay or straight, will form intimate relations that are full of rage toward others who in his mind threaten to engulf or bind him. Likewise, any child, heterosexual or homosexual, who has a distant, uninvolved, or unloving father will form relations with other men that are suffused with suspicion and rage. A gay man whose father rejected him, whether out of anxiety or because of his son's atypicality, may find that his relations with other men are disturbed. He may be inhibited by a fear of rejection and by rage at the partner, who, he believes, will inevitably injure him emotionally.

Some men may have more of a neuroendocrine predisposition toward feminine behavior and appearance than others. [30] Whether a child is homosexual or heterosexual, his "feminine" behavior or appearance may cause parents and peers in our society to respond to him in particularly cruel and rejecting ways, affecting his capacity for trust and intimacy. Cultural factors facilitate or inhibit the expression of sexual behavior. In our society, of course, all homosexual behavior is labeled "bad" and "feminine," influencing the nature of a gay man's self-perception and the manner and comfort with which he expresses his sexual behavior.

In *The Symposium*, Plato gives Aristophanes a humorous speech about the nature of man and the origin of his sexuality. Originally, man was a rounded whole. There were three sexes: male, female, and hermaphrodite, each bisected by Zeus as a punishment for man's pride. The sex of the loved one is dictated by the nature of the whole to which that individual originally belonged. Each half yearns for the half from which he has been separated.

Like all forms of love, homosexuality remains mysterious and eludes our total understanding. Like all forms of love, it is a longing for a lost attachment. That longing, for gay men, is usually for the father.

2

Childhood and
Early Homosexual Identity

MOST ADULT gay men state that their homoerotic attraction started somewhere between ages eight and thirteen or fourteen. Sometimes it is recalled as having "always been present." Almost all the gay men whom I have seen in psychoanalysis or in psychoanalytically oriented psychotherapy, though varying in their recollection of the age of onset of their sexual interests, report that, starting from about age four, they felt that they were "different" from their peers. They saw themselves as more sensitive than other boys; they cried more easily, had their feelings more readily hurt, had more aesthetic interests, enjoyed nature, art, and music, and were drawn to other "sensitive" boys, girls, and adults. Most of these men also felt they were less aggressive as children than others of their age, and most did not enjoy participating in competitive activities.[1] They report that they experienced themselves as being outsiders since these early childhood years.

Many adult gay men are unable to remember their earliest same-sex erotic feelings, fantasies, and impulses, but they sometimes recollect childhood behaviors and characteristics which they label as "different," or as "feminine." The clear recollection of being different acts often as a screen that hides childhood same-sex erotic fantasies, which they believed then and usually still believe were reprehensible.

Sexual memories are in the recesses of every patient's mind. They turn up eventually either as direct memories from child-hood or as indirect memories that can be reconstructed from the transference or from his current relationships, which are inevitably being influenced by them. Like the opposite-sex fantasies of the heterosexual child, the same-sex fantasies of the homosexual child shape the adult's attitude and behavior. Let's look briefly at the lives of three men and how certain childhood behavior was used by them to screen early repressed same-sex feelings.

When I first saw Alan in consultation, he was thirty-two years old and looked well muscled but somewhat tight and rigid. He had a small, neat mustache and gave the overall impression of being quite masculine. He initially came to me because he felt lonely and anxious and dissatisfied with his relationships. He seemed moderately depressed and said he was distressed over the breakup a month before of a year-long love affair. He spoke easily of his homosexuality in the initial sessions, but, while readily speaking of his attraction to other men, he also related how difficult it was to feel close to them. He had had a five-year relationship with one man which had been "tempestuous" and sexually one-sided. He had had more than one experience in which he had felt too much in the role of pursuer for his own comfort. Although being the pur-suer made him feel "sexually alive," and even more attracted to his lovers than when he was the pursued, it also made him feel unattractive, unloved, and unlovable.

During the early hours of our work together he spontaneously recollected that he had felt "different" from his peers during early childhood. He described this in part as "not liking to hit people or rough stuff. I seemed more sensitive than other kids. I never liked being demanding. I spent a lot of time playing the piano." He did not enjoy participating in the activities and many of the games of his male peers, and felt he was excluded because of this from some of their social activities. He grew up believing that his sensitivity, along with his love of nature and his love of music, and even his concern for the feelings of other people, were signs of his not being masculine, which in early adolescence he equated with being defective. Although peer recognition came readily during his adolescence because of his intelligence, good looks, and a proclivity toward muscularity, this did not ease his developing feeling that there was something very wrong with him. More than once he said to me, "I never could understand why I was selected for the Honor Society. When I was chosen, I actually thought they were talking about someone else and not me."

Alan's father was described as distant, a man of few words and fewer feelings. Although his father always earned a good living, Alan looked upon his work as demeaning. He accepted his mother's view that his father lacked ambition for not aspiring to managerial and executive positions rather than the hands-on work that he always enjoyed. Alan's mother was clinically depressed during much of his childhood, but she was the dominant force in the family and it was on her needs and wishes that most decisions centered. He felt he was favored by both his parents over a sister who was two years older than he. In his artistic and musical interests he perceived himself as being like his mother. In his acquiescence, nondemandingness, passivity, and emotional distance he saw himself as being more like his father.

Alan consistently treated me with a striking indifference that suggested a need to deny that I was of any importance to him. Although he came regularly to appointments and worked conscientiously, even after many months he seemed unconcerned and disinterested in what I said during these hours.

I pointed out to him that he had a need to keep me and other men in his life emotionally distant, and over time he became more comfortable in expressing feelings of curiosity and warmth. These changes in our relationship helped him to become more open with others, and he soon met a new lover, who was spontaneously and comfortably affectionate and tender. During this period of generally increasing ease with his own affectionate and sexual feelings, Alan began to recall sexual fantasies that he had when he was four about muscular comic-book heroes. He also remembered that from age nine he was attracted to other boys in his class. As these sexual feelings became clearer, he became less preoccupied with feelings of having been different as a child. He had less need to protect himself from old erotic feelings that were now becoming increasingly acceptable.

During this time, many of his therapy hours dealt with his longing for his father. He remembered that it was his father who would read him *Superman* and *Captain Marvel* comic books and that he felt warmth and pleasure while sitting on his father's lap. It became clear to both of us that his sexual interest and excitement over muscular comic-book heroes at age four were displaced and disguised expressions of his repressed sexual feelings toward his father.

Another young man, Benjamin, first sought help because of his low self-esteem, and his discontent with his work specifically and with his life in general. He readily acknowledged that he was homosexual, but, unlike Alan, in the earliest hours he frequently expressed the wish that he were not. He recognized that he was afraid of getting close to anyone, so that it was impossible for him to form a relationship, which, by and large, accounted for his intense loneliness. He, too, reported that as a child he had no interest in sports, that he was very interested in artistic endeavors, and that he cried easily, all of which isolated him from his peers. He had not enjoyed playing with either girls or boys of his own age, and he remained by himself a lot of the time. He, too, had felt "different."

He described his father as a large, dark-complexioned man, whom he saw as having been gruff and harsh but who was always available to him. He described his mother as being beautiful, narcissistically involved with herself, demanding, clinging and possessive.

During the first months of his analysis, Benjamin would not talk of any sexual experiences that had occurred before he was in college. During the second year, however, he spoke of sexual experiences that had occurred when he was twelve and was picked up by a college student who "taught" him to masturbate. Similar sexual encounters continued throughout his adolescence. As an adult his usual masturbation fantasies were of being picked up by dark, muscular men and being dominated by them, feelings similar to those he had as an adolescent when he was picked up by men in their twenties or thirties.

Benjamin had severe early injuries to his self-esteem because of his bond to a mother whom he perceived as being unable to love him and who used him to fulfill her own ungratified needs and ambitions. Consequently, his capacity to relate to others in a warm or empathic or loving manner was very limited. To a much greater degree than Alan, Benjamin remained very distant from me and others. He described feeling as if he were encased in plastic.

The first clear manifestation of erotic feelings toward me occurred after many years of analysis and was an expression of his wish to be dominated and sexually penetrated, feelings that terrified him. These wishes were soon accompanied by recollections of the great warmth and comfort he experienced while lying in bed with his father on weekend mornings. He gradually recalled childhood memories, which at first were hazy and then became clearer, of sexual thoughts about his father and about other boys his own age. These memories dated from about age four, at the time when, he reported, he felt that he was "different" from his peers. Benjamin's preoccupation with being different as a child lessened considerably, just as Alan's had, as he interpreted these early-childhood same-sex erotic memories.

I saw Carl for the first time when he was a first-year graduate student. He was a slender, clean-shaven young man, nice-looking but not conventionally handsome. He sought help because of his inability to become meaningfully involved with another man, because of his loneliness and his extremely low self-esteem. His sexual activity was confined to the bathroom of a public library and to pornographic bookstores, behavior he felt very guilty about. Like the men mentioned earlier, Carl also recalled that when he was seven or eight he had little interest in aggressive activities, that he was more sensitive than other boys, and that he enjoyed nature and aesthetic interests more than other boys his age—that he was "different." He was sometimes teased and mocked and cruelly excluded from parties by his classmates. He believed that this rejection by his peers was a sign that something was seriously wrong with him, and this rejection during his primary-school years so injured him that he initially accounted for his current low self-esteem on that basis alone.

Like Alan's and Benjamin's, his relation with me was at the beginning one of self-imposed emotional distance and mistrust. At times he would spontaneously mention that he was not attracted to "older men in their forties," feeling they were "lecherous" and would take advantage of him. He was mainly attracted to passive, androgynous-appearing young men, although his masturbation fantasies were almost consistently of powerful black men with large penises, or of being dominated. He had intense anxiety about anal sex and was often too tight to permit anal penetration, especially if he felt affection for his sexual partner.

He experienced slowly evolving and occasional feelings of warmth toward me that were at times accompanied by the wish to be dominated. At the same time he began to recall vague memories of sexual feelings toward boys in his class in the early years of grade school. His expanding early recollections also included the memory of childhood affection for his father and the suggestion of early sexual feelings toward him from about age four. His current sexual anxieties began to decrease as he gained greater awareness of these childhood sexual feelings and as he became less self-critical and condemning of himself for having them.

It has become clear to me from working with these and other gay men that homoerotic fantasies are usually present from at least the ages of four or five years. This period of development is analogous to the Oedipal stage in heterosexual boys, except that the primary sexual object of homosexual boys is their fathers.

It is most often the same-sex erotic fantasies centering on the father that initially make these children feel different from their peers. The child's perception of and response to these erotic feelings by themselves may account for such "atypical" behavior as greater secretiveness than other boys, self-isolation and excessive emotionality. Other traits that they soon label as being "feminine" may also be caused by identification with the mother or mother surrogate. Such characteristics usually develop as a way of attracting the father's love and attention, in a manner similar to the way the heterosexual boy may pattern himself after his father to gain his mother's attention. Some of the behavior considered to be gender atypical for the four-, five-, or six-year-old boy, such as his relative lack of aggressiveness and his greater compassion, sensitivity, or aesthetic sensibility, which may be a result of this identification, persists into adulthood. Other more overtly "feminine" behavior of some homosexual boys may disappear in adolescence and adulthood, because of the pressure for peer socialization.[2]

Not all societies have such a rigid concept of what is natural, what is acceptable, and what is typically male and female. Many American Indian cultures tend to have more tolerance for atypicality in childhood. The berdache, for example, are androgynous or effeminate-appearing males who cannot or choose not to assume the conventional roles ascribed to males in their culture. While the position of the berdache varies from society to society, these children, who are nonconforming in both behavior and appearance, are accepted and treated with special regard. They are given not only a secure place in the society but often a privileged and sacred role, such as that of shaman or the person from whom the shaman seeks advice. Or they may be assigned certain ceremonial tasks such as preparing food or giving blessings.[3]

In our society, where male and female roles and behavior are rigidly defined at all developmental levels, conformity is prized and atypicality, particularly gender atypicality, is viewed with scorn and usually rewarded with humiliation and derision. Homosexual youngsters of four, five, and six, particularly those who show any variance from what is considered typically male, develop a sense that they are outsiders or feminine. This early self-perception may lead in later childhood to secretiveness and isolation. Such behavior in turn frequently affects the response of peers and may result in further social isolation and unhappiness.

3

Fathers and Their Homosexual Sons in Childhood

THE MAJORITY of gay men, unlike heterosexual men who come for treatment, report that their fathers were distant during their childhood and that they lacked any attachment to them. Reports vary from "my father was never around, he was too busy with his own job," to "he was victimized by my mother, who was always the boss in the family," to that of the abusive, unapproachable father.

Occasionally patients describe fathers who were present, but they portray them as having been uninvolved. I doubt that these descriptions are more frequent in my population of patients than in the general population, since similar observations have been made by others about the fathers of gay men who are not patients.[1]

I have been impressed by the similarity between the recollections of gay men about their fathers and the reports of heterosexual men about their mothers. It appears that gay men's memories of their fathers, like those heterosexual men have of their mothers, are often caused by defensive distortions arising from the anxiety the adult feels about his early erotic attachment to the parent. Gay men distance themselves from their fathers in their memory in order to avoid recognition of this erotic attachment and of their sexual arousal in early childhood.

It is important to be able to distinguish between the nature of the actual parenting gay men have had and the retrospective perceptions and distortions of the nature of this parenting. Most analysts who work with heterosexual men would consider the distorted perceptions about both the mother and the father that are caused by repression to be important, but the same emphasis has not been applied in clinical work with gay men. It is the analysts' acceptance of the adult's perception of his father that has been responsible for the unwarranted conclusion that the presence of a "constructive, supportive, warmly related father precludes the possibility of a homosexual son."[2]

The reason for such conceptual errors appears clear. Since homosexuality is regarded as a pathological phenomenon and therefore not analogous to heterosexuality, the search for environmental and familial pathogens has led to incorrect attributions of poor parenting rather than to a recognition of the normal defensive distortions that occur in the perception of every human being of his or her parents. The search for developmental aberrations in a gay man's early life has prompted the discovery of what may not in fact be present. This inadequacy of conceptualization and the distortion of clinical perception are the result of the heterosexual bias of our society, which affects most clinicians in their work with gay men.

There are additional reasons for the perception by gay men that their fathers were not available to them in childhood, besides the defensive distancing from early erotic feelings. There are some fathers who really are absent or distant, due to their relationship with their spouse, preoccupation with work, or emotional limitations. These, of course, are factors which influence the fathers of heterosexual sons as well as of homosexual sons.

Particular to the childhood of homosexual boys, however, is that their fathers often become detached or hostile during the child's early years, as a result of the child's homosexuality. Fathers usually perceive such a child as being "different" from other boys in the family, from themselves, or from their sons' peers. These boys may be more sensitive, have more aesthetic interests, may not be involved in competitive activities, and may be more seclusive than heterosexually inclined boys. This may lead both to the father's withdrawal and to his favoring an older or younger male sibling who appears to be more sociable, more conventional, more "masculine." Some of the fathers of homosexual boys either consciously or unconsciously recognize that their sons have both a special need for closeness and an erotic attachment to them. These fathers may withdraw because of anxiety occasioned by their own homoerotic desires, which are usually unknown to them.

In my experience, then, the frequent description by a gay man of his father as detached, absent, or hostile stems from the need to distort the memory of his early erotic attachment to his father, and from the actual withdrawal of the father from his homosexual son once he becomes aware that his child is not acting like other boys his age or because of his own anxiety over the intensity of his son's attachment to him.

The withdrawal of the father, which is invariably experienced as a rejection, may be a cause of the poor self-esteem and of the sense of inadequacy felt by some gay men. It is also an important reason why some gay men have difficulty forming loving and trusting rather than angry and spiteful relationships.[3]

Important to and ubiquitous in the love life of adult gay

men is the persistence of an early erotic attachment to the father and a need to defend against these feelings. This attachment has a profound influence on the gay man's later love life.

Childhood Romance with the Father

I have mentioned Benjamin, who was twenty-seven when he entered analysis and who came to see me because he was depressed and dissatisfied with his life. He reported that he had been sexually attracted to other boys from about age eight, but he was extremely anxious about his homosexuality because of his inability to form any gratifying relationships. Benjamin's sexual activities centered almost exclusively on hustlers whose attentions he could control with money and with whom intimacy was never possible. He was often in physical danger, since many of these hustlers were addicts, and as time went on, there was the even more significant danger of contracting AIDS, a risk to which he seemed oblivious.

Benjamin's description of his family appeared to fit some of the conventional formulations about the genesis of homosexuality. His mother was reported as binding him to her and relying on his dependency for her own unsatisfied needs and gratification. He initially spoke of his father as having been cold, emotionally distant, and often absent because of his preoccupation with work.

During the first two years of his analysis, Benjamin appeared to be indifferent both to the analysis and to me as his analyst. He was distant and formal in his approach to our work together. During the third year of his analysis, he started to have recollections of having had homoerotic feelings for other boys when he was about four or five. And then his dreams and the nature of his relationship with me began to change.

This change was initiated by the following dream: "I'm on a roof with these people. They first look pale or white and then they become more distant. They begin to move across the roof in patterns that I find exciting." He made associations to people who had been in concentration camps and had been freed at the end of the war. He thought of someone he knew who he felt was free of his "hang-ups" and was "living in the moment." He then thought of his father and me as oppressors like Nazis, and of meeting someone in a bar the night before whom he found attractive. "He reminded me of a thief I once knew. I was very turned on by both of them." After thinking about his father's questionable business dealings, he wondered whether he had ever been "turned on" by his father when he was a child.

A few days later he had the following dream: "A horse comes between me and Fred [his boss, for whom he had considerable affection]. Fred reaches up and cuts the sheets near the pillow to cover the horse up." He remembered that Fred is the name of his father's brother. He then recalled sleeping in the same room with his parents when he was a child. His mother slept "like a horse" and usually lay between him and his father. As he was telling me this, he had a vague sense of sexual arousal and of having felt some attraction for his father, when he was about four. He was able to recollect feeling "warm" when he slept next to him. Within a few weeks, father-like smells and voices began to evoke sexual-like feelings and sensations in him. He began to recall certain of his father's appealing qualities—exuberance, intelligence, enthusiasm, and, at times, warmth. In his relationship with me there appeared for the first time some erotic thoughts and feelings, including the wish at times to fellate me or for me to penetrate him anally.

As his perception of his father and then me began to change, his relations with other men also began to change. He gradually

became better able to develop a capacity for sexual responsiveness and intimacy. A few months later he met his first lover. But the closer he felt both to his lover and to me, the more depressed he appeared, the more anxious he became, and the more preoccupied he was with physical complaints. Some of his intense anxiety had to do with the complicated and difficult relationship with his mother, which was reevoked by any closeness. Other aspects of his anxiety, however, stemmed from his repressed erotic feelings for his father. While in previous sexual contacts that were casual or anonymous he could be anally penetrated or do the sucking, now the evocation of these desires in the intimate relations with his new lover and in his relationship with me, combined with memories of his feelings for his father, made him feel extremely anxious. He became convinced that I was growing more distant because he was having more sexual feelings and because I was being made anxious by his sexual feelings for me. This perception was both a projection of his own anxiety and an early recollection of his father. He recalled his father's rejection, saying, "I think he knew I was in some way attracted to him, perhaps even that I was in love with him, and then he withdrew."

This brief account cannot capture the complexity or subtlety of the many determinants of any feeling or behavior that became clarified during the course of analytic work. I use it simply to highlight Benjamin's deeply repressed and powerful erotic love for his father from early childhood. The repression of these erotic feelings was an important factor in his defensively distancing himself from other men. As our work together progressed and Benjamin understood more about the nature of his early erotic feelings for his father and about his need to remember him as cold and uncaring in order to push these feelings away, he also began to recall and to let himself experience more of his father's warmth, acceptance, and love. His relations with other men subsequently improved significantly, ushering in his successful attempt to find a lover.

The history of another young man further illustrates how the repression of erotic desire for the father in early childhood may contribute to the inhibition and distortion of a gay man's love for other men as adults, making it difficult to form intimate, close attachments. Edward started treatment with me when he was twenty-four because he was moderately depressed, a depression that stemmed in part from his loneliness. He had little conscious anxiety about his sexuality, feeling that he had "always been homosexual." He recognized that in early adolescence he had been attracted to certain teachers. He had his first sexual encounter when he was about fifteen, and had had a few short-term relations since that time, but these attachments never seemed to work out. He very seldom had sex outside of a relationship, but these relations were always short-lived, because he rapidly grew bored and dissatisfied and experienced little passion. If a man evoked his passion, he became disinterested in going out with him, feeling there was something wrong or "lower-class" about the sexual excitement.

Edward's mother was described as being loving and intelligent. He was always close to her, but he did not feel that she was binding or intrusive. His father was perceived as being remote, opinionated, and somewhat domineering. Edward expressed considerable disdain for him. There was a clear similarity between his feelings toward other men and the disdain he felt toward his father.

At the beginning of treatment, he recollected an incident when he was eight and was fondled by an older man. Initially he recalled this experience with great disgust and remorse and anxiety, but during his third year of treatment he recollected that there had been some excitement during the encounter.

A few weeks later he began to recall the sexual arousal he had experienced when he saw his father's penis. Thereafter Edward felt less inhibited and was more interested in having sexual contact with other men.

The sexual encounter when he was eight, frightening as it was, served as a screen for his early erotic interest in his father. As the repression and denial of his childhood recollections of erotic feelings gradually lessened, Edward's sexual fantasies became much more easily acknowledged and his sexual feelings in general became more readily and actively expressed.

Both these cases give something of the flavor of the childhood romance that gay men have with their fathers. Defenses against these erotic feelings may lead to a distortion of the gay man's perception of other men and to a fear of intimacy and may be the most important psychological cause of inhibited and impoverished relations in adulthood.[4]

Withdrawal of the Father

As was previously mentioned, the fathers of homosexual sons may withdraw because they perceive that their sons are too closely attached and attracted to them for the father's own comfort, or because they feel that their sons are unacceptably "different."

Glen's father was a laborer who had ambivalent aspirations for his children. On the one hand, he seemed to want them to surpass him; on the other hand, he appeared to be envious of their accomplishments. Glen was an articulate, intelligent, verbal, precocious child, one mark of his difference in a family where the parents were intelligent but uneducated. He also was "different" in many of the ways described before: not greatly interested in aggressive activities, quite sensitive, somewhat seclusive, and involved in aesthetic and artistic endeavors. He felt that his first same-sex fantasies occurred "very early," but it is not clear how early. He recollected that they started while he was still preadolescent, from about age eight or nine.

Glen entered analysis in great conflict about his father, proclaiming his hatred for him. His life, Glen felt, had been scarred by his father's severe rejection of him. When Glen told his parents he was homosexual, his enraged father had proclaimed, "I always hated you." Until recently, after more than five years, he had refused to see Glen or allow him in his house. Glen was devastated at the thought that he could never win his father's love and attention.

During the course of analysis, it seemed clear that the father withdrew from Glen after some period of early closeness. It was after a younger brother was born that the father shifted his interest from Glen to the new son.

Glen described his father as liking to appear very masculine but at the same time having a flair for the dramatic and the histrionic. On one or two occasions, he enjoyed taking a woman's role in local theatrical productions. Glen believed that his father's withdrawal was to some degree associated with his own anxiety about latent homoerotic feelings he might have had, possibly along with jealousy over my patient's closeness to his mother. The anger and mutual antagonism each apparently felt toward the other had evolved because of Glen's rage at his father over his withdrawal and rejection. The way this young man vented his hurt and anger was by subtly and at times not so subtly demeaning his father.

The father's rejection was extremely harmful to Glen's sense of self-worth and self-esteem and was largely responsible for the anxiety he felt when he met a man he liked. He anticipated that any relationship would wind up in disaster and rejection, like that with his father. This interfered with his capacity to form a close, loving, and responsive attachment to another man.

Carl's father had also withdrawn from him because he perceived his son was "different." Carl was in analysis for six years, entering treatment because of his self-disgust, ambivalence about his sexuality, and problems with intimate attachments. He could not enjoy sex within a relationship but had frequent casual sexual encounters. He initially perceived his father as having always been distant, and he was disdainful of his perceived lack of strength and subservience. Repressed erotic wishes and fantasies centering on the father were reflected in his dreams and fantasy life.

In the early years of his analysis Carl complained of his mother's withdrawal from him at the time of the birth of his younger brother, when he was three and a half. Later, however, he became acutely aware that his father had also become particularly remote at that time. He began to talk about his father's favoring this brother, who was more conventionally masculine.

Withdrawal of the father in favor of another, usually younger, more conventionally masculine male sibling, or even a daughter, is frequently noted by gay men, as it was by these two. Rage at and rivalry with such a sibling often hide fury at the father for the rejection. Erotic feelings toward the father may also be covered up by rage at a brother or sister.

Gay Men and Their Mothers

Although I am emphasizing the special importance of the relationship with the father, I do not minimize the importance of the primary attachment that any human being—straight or gay, male or female—has with the early care-giving, nurturing mother. All relations, especially intimate ones, are profoundly influenced by the nature of this earliest relationship, most particularly by the sense of security and love, comfort and caring, which affect self-esteem by conveying a sense of well-being to the child.

Unlike the generally consistent manner in which gay men describe their fathers, they depict their relations with their mothers in a variety of ways. Those men who have a positive sense of themselves and their sexuality usually describe their mothers as having been "good enough." Gay men may also be envious of and competitive with women, a feeling that they are often not aware of which originates in the rivalry with the mother for the father's attention. The description some gay men give of their mothers as being overbearing or binding, or as keeping them from their fathers, at times stems from anger at and envy of her closeness to the father.

My work with Carl illustrates this point. Early in therapy he described his mother as having come between him and his father. Much later he in fact remembered that she had encouraged them to do more things together. He recalled this only after he came to understand his unrequited longing for his father and his considerable anger at his mother for her easy access to him.

Some of a gay man's closest friendships throughout his life may be with women. It is not unusual to hear someone express the feeling that he is more comfortable with his female friends than his gay friends, or that they can understand him better, or even that he can more easily share intimate details of his life with them.

There is often an underlying bond with women that is based on a mutual attraction to other men, a bond initially shared with the mother. In common pursuit of the father, a homosexual child of four, five, or six may even assume some of her attributes and characteristics. The mutual bonding and closeness sometimes continue into adulthood and extend to other women.

Erotic Attachment to the Father in Adults

How do gay men express the effect of their persistent but usually conflict-ridden and repressed erotic attachment to their fathers? Benjamin had a proclivity as an adult to feel sick and helpless. He recalled that as a child his sickness seemed to overcome his father's self-preoccupation and to attract him away from the mother. On occasion he would feign sickness to get his father to take care of him as he cared for Benjamin's mother. As an adult, his bodily concerns and frequent somatic complaints were motivated by the same unconscious desire: to get his father to take care of him.

Jim entered analysis because of ambivalence about his sexuality and because of depression and anxiety. If a friendly or attractive man liked him, he felt turned on, but then he would begin to hate himself and feel foolish and repulsive. He would say that, "in the arms of a cold man, I wouldn't feel this way." Of course, such an attitude in love and sexual matters led to no intimacy and to unsatisfying sex.

On one occasion, while on vacation, Jim had noticed a father and son enter the dining room. He remembered that he felt more strongly attracted to the father than to the teenage son. He became uncomfortable, acknowledging that he had always wanted to be "daddy's little girl." And he began to recognize that when he felt foolish and repugnant he also felt he was being "like a woman," to which he connected his feeling helpless and wanting to be taken care of by other men. He recalled that his father liked to take care of people and that his mother frequently put herself in that position vis-à-vis the father. Jim had fantasies that if he were a girl like his mother, both his father and I would like him better. He wanted to be "daddy's little girl," not because he felt he was a threat and wanted to appease him but in order to belong to him.[5]

As I have said before, there is no evidence to suggest that early aberrant mothering causes those identifications with the mother that are traditionally regarded as the major determinant of homosexuality in men. Identification with the mother may, however, affect the nature and quality of the adult's sexual relationships. For example, such identification, if motivated by the erotic desire for the father in the homosexual child, may contribute to a gay man's interest in being passive and to his desire to be dominated rather than being more aggressive and assertive. Anxiety and guilt over these passive inclinations may at times inhibit sexual desire.[6]

Benjamin felt that he was "sick" and was filled with self-loathing when he grew close to a man after years of almost exclusive sexual activity with hustlers. The closer he felt, the more disgusted his sexual feelings and impulses made him. He was responding by and large to his anxiety over his early and persistent erotic feelings for his father. Any close relationship evoked these longings, making him momentarily feel "like a woman." Only with hustlers, whom he saw once or twice and whom he could control with money, could Benjamin permit himself to be the passive recipient of anal sex. In an on-going relationship, where his warded-off desires for the father could not be successfully repressed and denied, his passive sexual desires made him anxious and frequently impotent.

It was only with great difficulty that Edward could talk at all about his fantasies of passive sexuality. He felt anguished and disgusted by desires that he described as "girl-like." Most of Edward's sexual fantasies were about being the recipient of anal sex, but he found the "feminine" feelings associated with these fantasies so repugnant that he could only occasionally permit himself that sexual pleasure. As the early erotic longings for his father became clearer to him, his conflict about this type of sexual activity lessened.

Of all my patients, Carl was perhaps the most terrified of his passive sexual fantasies. Although he fantasized about men with large penises who might have anal sex with him, he was always too tight to permit this to occur. Random and anonymous sexual encounters, described as "compulsive" and "frantic," were in part motivated by his desire to avoid the passive feelings evoked by any intimate, warm, loving relationships. He was repulsed by his passive-receptive desires, and he believed that anyone who was close to him would hate him for them as well. During the course of his analysis, as these passive anal wishes became connected in his mind with his early desires for his father, the conflict and self-destructiveness diminished.

Identification with both parents or parent surrogates is, of course, inevitable in all children, gay and straight. It is not an all-or-nothing proposition. Identification with the father, for example, causes many gay men to prefer a more active, dominant role in gay sex, even though the gay man may still desire a representation of his father as a sexual partner. These same gay men may as children have taken on characteristics of their mothers in order to attract their fathers. In fact, some of the most feminine-appearing gay men may prefer to be the active sexual partner, while the reverse may also be true.

Nor is it only an identification with the perceived passive sexual desires of the mother that evokes conflict in some gay men. Scott preferred being the inserter in anal sex, but at times became inhibited or impotent because of the connection he saw between his taking this active role and his father. His father had been abusive both to him and to his mother, and

Scott had an unconscious fear that, being like his father, he might harm his lover. To protect his lover, this young man would inhibit his passion.

Disguised, repressed, or denied erotic feelings for the father may constrain the sexual responsiveness of some gay men, just as the sexual responsiveness of heterosexual men may be inhibited by their repressed and warded-off desires for the mother. As gay men understand better the nature of these old but persistent sexual desires, their conflict lessens and they acquire a greater responsiveness and more flexibility in their sexual fantasies and behavior. They usually derive increased pleasure from passive sexual behavior, as well as from less conflict-ridden, more active sexual practices and desires. And they are better able to enjoy a panoply of sexual fantasies and to make less conflicted decisions about the type of sexual activity they wish to engage in and when.

4

Adolescence and
Young Adulthood of Gay Men

MOST PSYCHOANALYSTS regard adolescence as the period in which a "homosexually inclined" child is given a second chance to put aside his homosexuality with proper psychological guidance and to rework those early developmental experiences that have thwarted heterosexual development. I consider this attitude clinically harmful to the gay adolescent's self-esteem, a self-esteem that may already be burdened by past experiences of rejection by the father and by alienation from peers. The stage has been set from early childhood as to whether attraction is for a person of the same or the opposite sex. Attempting implicitly or explicitly to realign the gay adolescent's sexuality to the conventions and expectations of society only serves to reinforce his perception of himself as undesirable and of his sexuality as disgusting, contributing to later difficulties he may have in believing that sex and affection can exist in the same relationship. He may experiment with heterosexuality, just as the heterosexual adolescent experiments with homosexuality, but his fantasy life and his sexual impulses remain predominantly homosexual.

Every child enters adolescence with a burden of guilt from forbidden childhood erotic feelings and impulses. Adolescence is the anxiety-provoking time when a child attempts to place physical and emotional distance between himself and his parents, when the acceptance and values of peers become increasingly important, and when sexual impulses acquire new and often frightening power.

The development of sexual identity continues in adolescence with its consolidation through homoerotic fantasy, masturbation with homoerotic imagery, sexual attraction to other boys, and sexual experiences. This process normally leads in late adolescence to self-labeling, or "coming out" to oneself.[1] For the gay adolescent this developmental period may be particularly anguishing. He has usually entered adolescence with more sexual guilt than the heterosexual boy because he perceives that his sexual feelings and impulses are different from those of his family and peers. His self-esteem has often already been injured by the withdrawal of the father, by the rejection of other boys, by his perception and labeling of himself as "different," and by the internalization of society's prejudices and biases. These early experiences make him believe that his sexuality is immoral or disgusting and that he is either evil or sick. It is difficult for the gay adolescent to have sufficient self-regard to allow him to acknowledge without great pain and significant delay that he is homosexual.[2]

A good example of the sustained denial that can precede this acknowledgment comes from Alan's memory of his adolescence. Unlike many gay adolescents, Alan was popular in high school. He was masculine-appearing, good-looking, intelligent, and sensitive to the needs of other boys and girls. But Alan always felt like an outsider and remained aloof because of his perceived difference. He tried to "fit in" by dating one girl throughout high school. Because he was not sexually excited by her but felt obliged to attempt to have sex, he became agitated and sick before most dates. They never did have intercourse, and she broke off the relationship after several years.

He was not "turned on" to women, so he could not talk about sex with other boys without faking it. Moreover, his attraction to classmates and friends made him feel that there was something wrong with him and that he should not talk to anyone about his sexual feelings. Alan associated homosexuality with being effeminate, since that was the way homosexuals were portrayed in the movies and those were the only men he could readily identify as gay. Therefore, he did not believe that he was really homosexual. He thought that his sexual impulses were part of a passing phase, that these feelings would eventually disappear, and that the "proper" sexual desire would somehow, sometime in the future, replace his active homosexual fantasy life.

Alan's closest friend in college was gay. This friend wanted to have sex, and the attraction was mutual, but Alan could not associate his passion with a sexuality that remained unacceptable and therefore unnamed. "It was O.K. for him," he felt, "but not for me. You see, I was a liberal before I knew I was gay."

He fell in love in the first year of graduate school, when he was twenty-three. It was the power of this feeling that allowed him to recognize and acknowledge that he was, in fact, homosexual. This first sexual relationship was passionate, tempestuous, loving, and warm, and lasted over the next year or two. For some gay adolescents like Alan, falling in love is the only experience that can overcome the resistance and denial produced by previous years of alienation and self-disgust.

Another young man, Gregory, had an almost totally exclusive homoerotic fantasy life since early adolescence, and quite likely from early childhood. Reared in a Catholic family, he grew up believing that his homosexuality was a sin. He had two or three casual heterosexual experiences when he was sixteen, but they were not sexually or emotionally satisfying. He had several homosexual experiences over the next two years that were highly pleasurable but devoid of emotional significance. In spite of these experiences, he did not acknowledge that he was gay and, like Alan, he believed that it was a passing stage, part of a "tumultuous, rebellious adolescence." He tried to keep from having any emotional involvements with other boys which could jeopardize his relationship with his parents or which, he later told me, would have made him aware that he was, in fact, homosexual.

When he was twenty-six, he did meet a young man to whom he was attracted and he fell in love. He spent almost every evening and weekend with his lover, whom he grew to rely on for support and emotional gratification. Although he initially felt guilty, he began to function better at school, to feel more whole, and gradually to look more favorably upon himself. After a while he saw himself not only as gay but as healthy. For the first time he felt no remorse, no shame, no guilt. Falling in love enabled Greg to consolidate his homosexual identity. The self-affirming value of a mutual relationship over time cannot be overemphasized.

The experience of these two men is similar to that of many gay adolescents who acknowledge their sexual orientation only after a relatively sudden breakthrough of their denial and repression. They often describe this as an "ah-ha" experience. It is caused by a heretofore unaccepted sexual arousal pattern coming together with a sexual object. It feels like the pieces of an old puzzle falling into place. As Alan said, "Until then I had felt that I could never fall in love, that I had no sexual feelings, and that I never would, and that the feelings that I did have weren't what they should be." A sense of relief, well-being, and "rightness" follow.

In *Giovanni's Room*, James Baldwin captures the moment when he first recognizes his attraction to another man:

> I laughed and grabbed his head as I had done God knows how many times before, when I was playing with him or when he had annoyed me. But this time when I touched him something happened in him and in me which made this touch different from any touch either of us had ever known. . . . Then, for the first time in my life, I was really aware of another person's body, of another person's smell. We had our arms around each other. It was like holding in my hand some rare, exhausted, nearly doomed bird which I had miraculously happened to find. I was very frightened; I am sure he was frightened too, and we shut our eyes. To remember it so clearly, so painfully tonight tells me that I have never for an instant truly forgotten it.[3]

The consolidation of sexuality and the beginning of integration as part of a positive self-image does not usually occur as early in homosexual adolescents as it does in heterosexual boys. Childhood experiences, the internalization of social disapprobation, the wish to fulfill heterosexual cultural expectations, and the need for peer approval usually cause the homosexual adolescent to suppress or deny his sexuality with great vigor. Many gay adolescents "know" from childhood that they are homosexual, but the homosexual youth, entering adolescence with "the sin not to be named," comes equipped with many ways to deny and avoid this stigma.[4] Most straight adolescents enter this developmental stage feeling that their sexuality is on shaky ground, but they are able and proud to proclaim their heterosexuality and untried sexual prowess.

Not all gay adolescents have their first sexual experiences

within a relationship and those who don't may have difficulty later in bringing together affectionate feelings and sexuality.

> One day when I was eleven, I had a cold and ran out of Kleenex on the way home from a movie. So I went into the subway men's room when I got off the train and stood near a booth snatching toilet paper. I paid no attention to the man at the urinal who suddenly groped me while I blew my nose. I couldn't believe it: he looked just like anyone else. I pushed his hand away and fled the restroom. Halfway down the steps I stopped cold, immobilized at the sexual heat, did an about-face, paid another fare, and returned to the restroom. He was still there. I repeated my gestures and he repeated his, more tentatively this time. I did not resist. . . .
>
> That scene became typical. Fresh from the subway johns, I would nibble and sip and remember until it was time to collect my books for Hebrew school. While the other boys recited from the sacred Torah, I mused on my profane moments, vivid as the mixed smells of ammonia, perspiration, and semen. . . . Part of me hoped it was just a phase, that I would settle down and begin to enjoy girls. . . .
>
> I assumed homosexuality was entirely an issue of lust. I made efforts to ask questions when I could, but the men who did me were either uninterested in talk or unable to tell me anything that added to what I already saw. I could have done without such high seriousness, without the nasty thoughts of betrayal that did little for my pudgy self-esteem. Most of all, I could have done without the corrosive fantasies.[5]

Seymour Kleinberg's "coming out," initiated by an accidental sexual encounter and confirmed through a succession of random sexual experiences, was more gradual and took place earlier than that of the young men I have mentioned. His early casual sexual experiences could have made it difficult for him to bring together as an adult his longing for affectionate relationships and his perception that his sexuality was "entirely an issue of lust." These activities can grow ever more separated from warmth and affection as one learns to believe that sexuality is "corrosive."

There are many heterosexuals who have frequent random adolescent sexual experiences in which the sexuality is separated from the experiences of love and affection, but this is a more common experience for gay adolescents and is less defined by social class than it is for heterosexuals. Early experiences of feeling different, alienated, and rejected may all contribute to a conviction that one's sexuality is disgusting and to difficulty in sustaining a sense of self-worth in the face of normally strong sexual impulses. The interdictions of society have made public urinals and bathhouses the courting grounds of some homosexual adolescents. Stealth, secrecy, urgency, and the unclean are discovered when relationships are not sanctioned.

Injured self-esteem from internalized social prejudice may lead to very long delays in a gay man's recognition of his sexuality. Donald was in his late thirties before he was able to acknowledge his homosexuality to himself. He was aware of homoerotic fantasies in childhood and of being aroused by boys in grade school. His masturbation fantasies were almost exclusively homoerotic and his occasional adolescent "fooling around" with other boys was pleasurable. But he could not place himself in the group of people that he recognized as homosexual. He did not believe that he was like the homosexuals he heard spoken of with such disgust by his friends or like the effeminate men portrayed in the movies, so he became convinced that he was just "sick." In order to rid himself of his affliction, he began psychoanalysis shortly after entering graduate school. He was delighted that his analyst did not believe that he was homosexual and encouraged Donald's forays into heterosexuality. In some curious way Donald was even reassured that his analyst believed he was heterosexual enough to reinforce Donald's self-loathing over persistent homosexual impulses and masturbation fantasies. His analyst encouraged him over many years to understand the always present homosexuality as a defense against conflicted wishes to be heterosexual and against Donald's competitive, hostile wishes toward the father.

Largely to please his doctor, Donald married during this first analysis. He described being enormously anxious as he attempted to make love to his wife, and most of the time he was impotent, blaming his wife for his futile attempts to experience sexual excitement. He felt like an inanimate object, detached and unarousable, lonely and desperate. After just three years of marriage he separated from his wife, and later they were divorced. Because he felt increasingly desperate, hopeless, and worthless, he terminated this first treatment.

Donald immediately felt released from the confinement of his transference need to please his analyst. He described an internal sense of freedom which he did not fully comprehend. Within one month he had an anonymous homosexual encounter. This was quickly followed by the recognition that he was homosexual and by an enormous feeling of relief. For the first time in his life he felt that he was sexually vital and alive, rather than disembodied and separated from his feelings. The depression and the low self-esteem that had plagued him for many years began to lift spontaneously. He no longer needed to find himself sick or disgusting in order to suppress his homosexual fantasies. That it took him so long is a measure of his self-loathing and of the power of his childhood need to conform to his parents' expectations in order to please them.

In another analysis a few years later he focused on his rage at the first analyst, a rage that stemmed from his analyst's denial of his homosexuality, confirming to him his fear that he was never and could never be loved as the person he was. His second analysis was not long. Donald now knew who he was and that he wanted to establish a loving relationship with a man. The second analysis contributed to the consolidation of his homosexuality as part of his identity, mitigating the image he had of himself as being bad. There was a two-session follow-up four years after termination; at that time he had been involved for two years in a gratifying relationship, a relationship that, because it is loving, is in itself an important source of self-esteem for this man, as it is for everyone.

Many men do not "come out" to themselves with such suddenness. Some who have less need for peer recognition than Alan and less hunger for parental love than Donald may acknowledge their sexuality more gradually during their adolescence.

Edward, for example, felt depressed and generally uncomfortable when he started graduate school. His depression in some measure was associated with difficulties he had in dealing with rage at his rejecting father. He had a good relationship with his mother, who was described as intelligent, warm, and loving. He matter-of-factly acknowledged being gay during our first hour when he spoke of his relationships and of looking for, but not yet having found, the "right man." There was no ambiguity in his mind about the nature of his sexuality, but like every gay man, he had periods of regret, confusion, and even despair at times, about his sexuality.

At about twelve years of age he had become aware of his attraction to two of his teachers whom he had identified as being gay. His adolescent masturbation fantasies were rather consistently of a man lying on top of him, making him feel submissive and warm and cared for. He was aware of being turned on by some of his classmates and his teachers as well. When he was fifteen, he had a sexual experience with a man about twice his age. Although pleasurable, this sexual encounter was accompanied by some guilt and anxiety. His subsequent sexual experiences were progressively more pleasurable, and in his second year of college he acknowledged to himself that he was homosexual. There was no rush of relief, since he had suspected from the homoerotic nature of his masturbation fantasies and from the pleasure of his past sexual experiences that he was gay.

Although consolidation of sexuality begins with the recognition of homoerotic fantasies and of sexual attraction to other boys in early adolescence, it is the sexual experiences themselves in middle or late adolescence that usually lead to self-acknowledgment.

The sexual activity of gay adolescents can be distinguished from the homosexual activity of heterosexual boys. It has less of the accidental, intermittent, experimental quality of the straight adolescent's homosexual activity. It feels "real." It has a strong affective element, either the feeling of being in love or a longing for love with the sexual partner, or a drivenness that demands an object for fulfillment. This sexual activity resembles more the initial sexual encounters of heterosexual adolescents with girls than the sexual play of straight boys with other boys. Although heterosexual boys may certainly have powerful crushes on idealized older men or peers, these are not usually sexually acted on. When they are, a strong bisexual or homosexual orientation is almost certainly present. The heterosexual activity of homosexual adolescents has a quality of experimentation similar to the heterosexual boy's homosexual activity and, like it, is usually accompanied by a good deal of anxiety.

Impediments to the Integration of a Positive Sexual Identity

There are developmental impediments for homosexuals and heterosexuals alike that may interfere with the capacity to form intimate relations and, for gay men, may then impede the normal integration of a positive homosexual identity. Some types of early relationships with the mother commonly cause severe self-esteem impairment and evoke unmanageable rage, often turned inward into a self-defeating masochism. One type of mother who may set this process in motion sees the child simply as an extension of herself and will block his natural strivings for emotional and physical independence. For the narcissistically injured adult, anyone who has the potential to offer him comfort and gratification may become an object of contempt and scorn. He unconsciously seeks out unfulfilling relationships or unattainable men who repeat a humiliating sense of unacceptance and rejection from the parent. There are many types of early parent-child interactions that, over a period of years, may make intimacy in adolescence and adulthood inordinately difficult. But narcissistically wounded people, both homosexual and heterosexual, are frequent visitors at any analyst's office, and I will use two to illustrate this point.

Benjamin entered analysis at age twenty-seven because of a poor self-image. Early in adolescence he had frequent homosexual experiences with men who dominated him. By the age of thirteen he had acknowledged to himself that he was homosexual, and he claimed that he "always knew." Yet he spoke of his sexuality as though it were a foreign appendage that he would like to have excised. I was, in fact, the second analyst he saw; the first, whom he left after a few months, was well known for attempting to convert homosexuals to heterosexuals. Benjamin's self-hatred was in part expressed as a hatred of his homosexuality and was further manifested as disgust for other gay men. He went out of his way not to associate with other homosexuals, not to be seen on the street with men who could be identified as such, and would even at times speak to associates at work of "fags" or "queers" and of his dates with women.

How did this self-hatred and his homophobia develop? During his analysis it became clear that Benjamin could not tolerate the anxiety that was generated by being alone and feeling separated from his mother; at the same time he was enraged by his feeling of attachment to her. He regarded this attachment as harmful. Sensing her destructiveness and ambivalence toward him, and partly out of an unconscious identification with her hatred, he developed a self-destructive need for frequent dangerous random sexual contacts. He believed that his mother perceived him as an extension of herself and that she had never conveyed to him a sense of his own separateness. He had little capacity to feel lovable; he could not think about himself without either compensatory inflation or intense self-hatred. His homosexuality became a focus of aspects of himself that made him feel hated and hateful. He had no capacity to sustain a sense of himself as a good person in a society that was inimical to and censorious of his sexuality. These narcissistic injuries that evoked rage and masochistic behavior motivated the selection of unloving, potentially dangerous sexual partners and were, as well, determinants of the difficulties he had in loving other gay men.

After many years Benjamin was able to learn enough about

his rage at his mother and to accept his early and continued unconscious erotic attachment to his father so that he became better able to avoid turning all sexual encounters into self-punitive exercises (see Chapter 3). He met a young man with whom he fell deeply in love, and he gave up dangerous sexual activities with hustlers to devote himself to his lover. Their relationship was a source of enormous enhancement of his self-esteem. He stopped speaking of himself with disdain and disgust and no longer avoided the company of other gay men. Because he now felt more worthwhile and lovable, he was also able for the first time to obtain pleasure from work-related endeavors.

Carl had also sought therapy because of low self-esteem, but unlike Benjamin, he had wanted from the beginning of treatment to form a meaningful relationship and had the desire to improve this aspect of his life. Whereas Benjamin had had many sexual experiences as an adolescent, Carl had only a few incidental sexual experiences in his last two years of high school. In college he began to have sex, mainly anonymous, which continued during the early years of therapy. He was invariably attracted to men who were not attracted to him. If they were, he drove them away by complaining about them, being self-involved, or communicating his disinterest.

He had ambivalently acknowledged his homosexuality from about age eighteen; he told me how he had hated himself for being gay. He would occasionally speak of going to "one of those shrinks" who might be able to change him. This would occur after he had felt particularly close to me, when he became threatened by this closeness and his well-defended sexual feelings. Carl's low self-esteem was manifested to a large degree in his hatred of himself for being gay. Consequently, he was "closeted" both to other gay men and to heterosexuals as well.

Like Benjamin, he avoided being seen with gay men, fearing that his sexuality would be discovered by people at work or by friends of his family.

Carl's mother treated him as an extension of herself and in many ways indicated to him that her goals and gratifications were to be accomplished through his accomplishments, and that his failures and unhappiness would result in her grave disappointment. Because he had little sense of himself as a person separate from his mother's aspirations, he was very dependent on peer and social approval for his self-esteem. Censorious social attitudes toward his homosexuality weighed heavily upon him. His relationship with his hostile mother filled him with rage and self-hatred, eventually leading to the difficulty he had in permitting himself any pleasurable sexual activity in the context of a gratifying, loving relationship. As with Benjamin, his ungratifying relationships and the corrosive nature of his sexual activity contributed to the conviction that his sexual orientation was a sickness and to his failure to integrate it as a part of a positive self-identity.

Although the manner in which these men expressed their sexuality was partially a reflection of their maternal environment, there is no evidence that the mothers of these two young men caused their homosexual orientation. The theory that a pathological or close-binding mother causes homosexuality derives from the sample of gay men most psychoanalysts and psychiatrists have seen. Since gay men with impoverished self-esteem are more likely to want to have their sexuality changed, they are also likely to seek the help of traditional psychoanalysts who are advocates of the pathology of homosexuality and the desirability of such change. As both Carl and Benjamin grew increasingly capable of tolerating more nourishing relations, their self-esteem and their perception of themselves as gay men were in turn enhanced.

Socialization—Coming Out to Others

Coming out to other gay men normally follows self-labeling and self-recognition and begins in middle or late adolescence. This usually leads to homosocialization—that is, to friendships with other gay men and to varying degrees of involvement in gay social networks. Relationships that are mutual and loving, both sexual and nonsexual, are essential to the healthy integration of a homosexual identity, promoting a positive self-image. Such relationships assist in overcoming the feelings of alienation and despair that are so often caused by rejections by the father and by peers in childhood and early adolescence.

Fred is a twenty-year-old college junior. He has had sex on a couple of occasions with a classmate he fell in love with, but he doesn't feel ready for a relationship. Although at times he wishes he were straight so he would be better accepted by society, he is turned on by men only and readily acknowledges that he is gay.

As a child and young adolescent he experienced considerable rejection from peers because of his unconventional behavior, especially his consuming preoccupation with baroque music and his refusal to participate in competitive sports. He felt isolated, lonely, and depressed much of the time and very guilty about his homosexual longings. As a college freshman he became part of a group of gay friends to whom he came out. They were mutually supportive and the first peer group in which Fred felt he fitted. He enjoyed being able to talk about his sexual feelings and particularly, when with a friend, being able to acknowledge that he found someone he passed on the street "cute." These friendships and continuing associations with other gays made Fred feel less isolated, and the sexual feelings shared with others who were well regarded contributed to his enhanced self-image.

This developmentally important process of homosocialization has been given little attention by psychoanalysts. Some analysts have stated that "social acceptance" increases the difficulty any homosexual has in being motivated to seek treatment, by reducing the feeling that he is "ill"; it should therefore be discouraged.[6] Others believe that investment in the homosexual world compensates for maternal deprivation, that it may be an expression of rage, and that narcissism is more pervasive in those gay men who are involved in the gay community than in those who are sexually but not socially gay.[7] On the whole, analytically oriented psychotherapists have little understanding of the importance of these attachments for the enhancement of self-esteem. Although social psychologists have discussed these issues, some argue that the consolidation of a normal identity as a homosexual requires a total or nearly total involvement in a gay community.[8]

Coming out to other gay men and being socially involved is a necessary aspect of the integration of one's sexual orientation. It is a way of discovering the positive role models that are denied gay youth in our society and of countering the social stigmatization and isolation that may occur during adolescence as well as during childhood from early experiences with fathers and peers.[9] However, the degree and nature of homosocialization may be limited in our society by restrictive factors such as geography, vocation, and availability. A gay man in a rural area is obviously going to have much less opportunity for social contact with other gays. Similarly, some gay men marry before they identify themselves as gay. If they choose to preserve the relationship with a wife, they also may have less opportunity for continuing social relationships with gays.[10]

A man of my acquaintance illustrates some issues that may restrict homosocialization. He lives in a small Midwestern town where there are only a few gay men. He has three or four gay friends to whom he is "out" and whom he sees on his frequent business trips, and he has had some sexual relationships, a few of duration and warmth, from which he derives emotional as well as sexual gratification. He considers himself to be gay, but he is well integrated into a conventional social community and into a vocation which affords him considerable financial rewards and social support. He is out to no heterosexuals. Had he chosen to remain closeted from other gays or had he not permitted himself any gratifying sexual contacts or relationships, I would regard this as a developmental failure, perhaps suggestive of significantly impaired self-esteem. His decision not to come out to heterosexuals is a different matter, since it is based on a realistic appraisal of the social and vocational disruptions that could ensue. If he moved to a metropolitan area where he could experience consistency and congruence between his internal and his social life, he might be happier. But that, he believes, would involve more sacrifice of his vocational and social position than he cares to make. His compromise is for him the only viable one.

In contrast is Dr. Howard Brown's announcement of his homosexuality to some six hundred physicians at a conference on human sexuality in October 1973. Three years before, Dr. Brown had resigned as Health Commissioner of New York because he feared exposure of his homosexuality by the columnist Drew Pearson. Faced with perpetual anxiety about exposure, and having grown increasingly comfortable with himself as a gay man, Brown decided to make a public statement, which served the significant purpose of encouraging public dialogue on gay rights. It was Brown's increasing sense of self-assurance as a gay man and enhanced self-esteem that led to his public coming out, ending his fear of exposure.[11]

Coming out to family members is usually important for the

positive integration of sexuality. But this must also be deter-
mined by reality factors in the life of every gay man; the
inability to come out may not necessarily be symptomatic of
a disturbance in self-esteem. Scott has been openly gay for five
or six years, comfortably out not only to members of the gay
community but to selective members of his vocational community as well. He has lived with a lover for several years.
While some problems with intimacy and the expression of
aggression at times hinder him in his relationship with both
his lover and his colleagues, he is reasonably comfortable with
his homosexuality. He has known he was gay since early adolescence, and recognized that he was having same-sex fantasies when he was eight or nine.

Scott's mother is a beautiful but emotionally distant woman
with whom he has a cordial but distant relationship. His father
is a successful businessman, given to occasional abusiveness
during Scott's childhood. Both his parents defensively deny
any difficulties in their often troubled relationship in order to
protect their marriage, and, similarly, do not acknowledge any
problems in their relationships with their children.

Scott and his lover have become increasingly affectionate
around his parents, and both are included in family functions.
But the parents appear to ignore the fact that, even though
they live together and have done so for many years, they are
lovers. He gains enormous gratification from this relationship
with his lover and does not disguise it, but Scott has decided
not to confront his parents with his sexuality or to articulate
to them that he and his boyfriend are lovers. Such a confron-
tation, he feels, would be unnecessarily disruptive to his parents and to the relationship he and his lover have with them.
Tolerating his parents' denial that Scott and his boyfriend are
lovers, however, entails more ego strength and courage for
him than confronting them would. His coming out to the

family and challenging their long-standing defenses might place an unwanted and unnecessary strain on his relationship with his parents, whom he sees only infrequently.

On the other hand, a friend of mine has been unable to form any significant gay relationships and is unable to think of himself positively as a gay man. His unwillingness to come out to his parents has been a way of placing angry distance between himself and them. There is every indication that both his mother and his father know he is gay and would even welcome his speaking with them about it. His choice not to do so is a symptom of his continuing failure to integrate his sexuality, of his need to maintain emotional distance from them, and is an expression of his rage toward them.

Edward, whom I have mentioned before, is quite comfortable with most aspects of his sexuality, except for conflict about his desire to be sexually passive, which at times interferes with his capacity for closeness and sexual enjoyment. He is equally open both with gay and with heterosexual friends. He is also totally open with his parents and siblings, with whom he has a close relationship. The process of coming out to parents and siblings has enhanced his self-esteem because of the acceptance, warmth, and reassurance of his family.

Some gay men marry because of their inability to accept themselves as gay. Because of their low self-esteem, they need to disguise this fact from themselves and others. Some who have previously denied or repressed their homosexuality do not discover until they are in a marriage that they are in fact gay. Most marriages between homosexual men and straight women are, in one way or another, the result of pressure for social conformity, though love and regard for the partner may also be present.[12] If the relationship is viable and it is important to the gay man to stay in the marriage, then coming out to the wife seems to be essential to the continuing integration of a positive self-image, regardless of the circumstances in which the marriage was entered. The timing of this disclosure depends upon such factors as the age of children, the duration of the marriage, the nature of the relationship, and personality characteristics of the spouse. Respect for the partner mandates that realistic options be considered and decisions be made together which permit both the man and the woman to continue to grow and lead fulfilled lives. Remaining in a marriage, however, may make it difficult for a gay man to integrate his sexuality fully into a positive gay identity; it makes it hard, and often impossible, for him to enter into a same-sex relationship in which he can be loved in a sustained and nourishing manner.

The development of a gay identity, which begins in the earliest years of childhood with same-sex erotic fantasies, usually carries with it, in our culture, the burdens of guilt and self-loathing that may impede or delay its consolidation and integration. Social stigmatization is particularly damaging to the adolescent and young adult because of the importance of peer acceptance in the task of separation from parents. Such stigmatization and the internalization of social bias often lead to further lags in the formation of a healthy sexual identity by encouraging conformity to prevailing social conventions such as marriage and to the denial of inherent sexual and attendant psychological and social needs.

5

AIDS: The Development
of Healthy Gay Men
and Homophobia

LATE IN 1984 I was asked by a college student if the AIDS epidemic was interfering with the ability of gay men to come to terms with their sexual identity. At that time I was just beginning to see victims of the epidemic in my practice. I was preoccupied with my own pain in working with the dying young and with the treatment issues that had begun to arise, so I had not given much thought to that point. Since then it has become increasingly clear that the AIDS crisis has, indeed, had a profound psychological affect on healthy gay men.

It is not possible to understand this without imagining how a homosexual adolescent or young adult feels when he reads that gay men are responsible for the spread of AIDS, or how assaulted he is by the increasingly frequent public outcries for mandatory testing, against the advice of public health officials, and by the possibility of further assaults on his civil rights and liberties. Most gay men experience these occurrences as a thinly disguised expression of social hatred.

The AIDS epidemic is thus adding another dimension to the self-esteem problems of gay men in our society that arise from the complexities of their development. Some healthy young adults may now perceive themselves as potential carriers of death, and others have become severely anxious about contracting the disease.

It is normal for all young adults, homosexual and heterosexual alike, to experiment sexually and examine the expression of their sexuality within and outside of relationships. The AIDS epidemic and increasing homophobia are producing developmental lags in some young gay men by adding to the perception that their sexuality is sinful, sick, or simply a matter of lust. It has caused some men to be afraid to express themselves as gay, depriving these young adults of the kind of experimentation necessary to understand themselves as men capable of a full and responsive sexuality in close and mutually loving relationships.

Jeffrey, who is twenty-four, had a few sexual experiences before the onset of AIDS and was, when he saw me for a consultation, in great conflict about his homosexuality. This was due both to fear of AIDS and to his mother's strong disapproval of his being gay. Since he had always sought to please her and lived his life as he felt she wished him to, his sexual activity had been limited to solitary masturbation and an occasional instance of mutual masturbation which had last occurred several years ago. Jeffrey was furious at his father, whom he perceived as being uninvolved and rejecting. As he spoke, it became clear that in all areas of his life he expressed rage at both his parents by spitefully withholding pleasure from himself. He articulated the fantasy that if he suffered, they suffered.

With the onset of AIDS, he ceased what limited sexual activity he had previously permitted himself. His fantasy life became less vivid, as did his sexual desire. He was feeling increasingly guilty about his homosexuality and bad about himself for being gay. To convince me of the rapacious sexual appetite of gay men and their lack of social concern, he quoted some of the comments made about homosexuals by a conservative New York columnist. Jeffrey obviously had always had conflicts about his sexuality as a result of his relationship with both his parents before AIDS, but the epidemic, his feelings about it, and the prejudice he was experiencing added to his conflict and had brought to a near-total halt his development as a man capable of a loving and responsive sexuality.

Another young man who readily acknowledged he was gay sought a consultation because he had never had sex. His attraction patterns, daydreams, and fantasies were totally homoerotic. Since the onset of the epidemic about two years before, he had even stopped masturbating. He had become concerned, from newspaper and television reports, that homosexuals were "on the prowl" for sex. He had grown so guilty about his sexuality that he permitted himself no sexual outlet at all; he was perpetually frustrated and increasingly depressed. His description of his family life was somewhat similar to Jeffrey's, and, as in his case, the intense fear of AIDS was an expression of his rage at both his parents turned masochistically against himself.

Yet another young man whom I saw in intensive psychotherapy illustrates in more detail how the AIDS epidemic may interfere with a homosexual's development. I first saw Seth early in 1984. He sought help because of severe inhibition in his sexual activity. Although attractive and intelligent, Seth believed that he was unattractive, especially his hips and buttocks. He would not remove his clothes in front of other men and so had no sexual contact during his first two years of college.

When I saw him for the first time, at the age of nineteen, he readily acknowledged that he was gay. He had never had sex with a woman, and his sexual fantasies were almost exclusively homosexual. He was aroused by boys in his class, but hated the idea of being attracted to anyone, finding it humiliating. He had been his mother's favorite until the birth of his younger sibling, when he felt abruptly displaced, humiliated, and rejected by her. He felt that his father had been inattentive to him, did not protect him from his mother's unpredictable moods, and was more expressive and loving with the younger child. His parents fought a good deal, and the more distant his father became because of these family difficulties, the more rejected Seth felt. As a child he had developed certain identifications with his mother, such as vocal mannerisms, which were designed to attract his father, but these, along with the fact that he did not like aggressive sports and enjoyed spending time by himself, drove his father further away.

The dual rejection by both parents made him feel injured and worthless. It was anger over these rejections which was largely responsible for his unwillingness to give himself emotionally or sexually to anyone and which made him vindictive and contemptuous of any man who appeared to be interested in him.

At the beginning of his therapy Seth would talk of his homosexuality as a "horror," and of his being "sick." He spent much of his free time alone in the university's library and had become well versed in those psychoanalytic ideas about homosexuality that reinforced his perception that he was, indeed, sick and perverse. Later in the therapy he began to recognize that it was not his homosexuality that revolted him but those characteristics in himself, such as his hips and thighs, which he felt were "feminine." These features were largely displacements of repressed erotic feelings for his ambivalently longed-for father (see Chapter 3).

As publicity about AIDS increased, Seth found reason to isolate himself further. The fear of contracting AIDS became a way of projecting his rage: he became convinced that someone was going to give him the disease. My efforts to help him understand that he was using the epidemic to deal with his own hostile impulses were largely futile. When I pointed out to him that neither his current behavior nor his fantasies suggested that he was going to engage in unsafe sex, he became furious and accused me of being unwilling to protect him from the illness, of exposing him to disease and death.

Seth dealt with rage at his parents by experiencing it as the projected danger of contracting AIDS from another gay man. The epidemic provided the necessary rationalization for totally inhibiting his sexuality. His anxiety and panic kept him from ever engaging in any intimacy that might cause him to feel that he could be harmful to another man. His fear of AIDS also kept him from having relationships, which he was convinced would bring him the same rejection and inflict the same humiliation that he had experienced from his mother and his father. It had become impossible for him to have the kinds of sexual experiences that all young people, homosexual and heterosexual alike, need to affirm their sense of sexual identity. Lacking that experience and freedom, Seth grew increasingly out of touch with the potentially self-affirming force of his passion and love.

Most gay men, as their sexual desires become less repressed and less conflict-ridden, acquire greater responsiveness and more flexible homoerotic fantasies and behavior. When sexual behavior is inhibited, as it was in Seth, and the underlying causes of the inhibition are uncovered, there is then a freer expression of sexual feelings and behavior. Seth's anger at me for supposedly encouraging him to engage in sexual behavior that might kill him gave me an opportunity to help him understand something about the early roots of his sexual inhibition and rage. It also provided me with the opportunity to acknowledge the real danger of AIDS and to educate him about safe sex.

This didactic attitude is not usual in a psychoanalyst or analytically oriented therapist. But these are not usual times, and I do not wait for patients to tell me about having unsafe sex before I assume an educational role; not when a fatal disease can be acquired through one such encounter. Helping patients first to clarify their conflicts and then suggesting caution may, of course, evoke further conflict about fantasies and desires. When this occurs, these conflicts must be further analyzed. But in fact my efforts to educate have not seemed to evoke further conflict on sexual issues, or self-defeating behavior during periods of negative transference. Because of the grave risk, my intervention has generally been considered thoughtful and caring. If the risks were not so great, such efforts to educate might well be regarded by many patients as moralistic or controlling and would therefore likely be used in self-injurious ways when they were angry.

The fear of AIDS has contributed specifically to the conflict some gay men feel about their receptive anal desires. This is illustrated by a man who started therapy in 1980, when he was twenty-two. One of his complaints was of intense anxiety about being gay, specifically about his desire to be anally penetrated, which had never occurred. This anxiety was symptomatically expressed as his being too tight to permit penetration. In 1982, after he read about the growing epidemic, his conflicts around his passive sexual wishes were more frequently expressed as a fear of contracting the disease and less frequently as anxiety over being too tight. In the next year it became clear that the suppression of these receptive sexual fantasies that he now perceived as dangerous because of AIDS led to their being expressed in other ways that were dangerous to him. For example, he began to invite men whom he perceived as menacing back to his apartment for "safe" sex. The receptive anal sexual fantasies and desires, which contributed to his feeling that he was bad and deserved to be punished, led to his unconscious wish to be injured by these strangers.

The AIDS epidemic contributed to his perception that his homosexuality was "perverse" and unhealthy and made it extremely difficult for him to express himself within a relationship. He had only random sexual encounters, because he was convinced that his sexuality was, in effect, a nighttime activity that did not belong within a relationship. This young man used the crisis as a rationalization for his anxiety about intimacy and for sadistic fantasies that were evoked in him by intimacy. It was a rationalization that effectively interfered with his development, not to mention his physical health. The epidemic removed his conflict from the internal and intrapsychic to the external, making it impossible for him for the time being to overcome his impoverished self-esteem, the result of earlier rejections and internalized homophobia, by experiencing the corrective love that a relationship can provide.

Let us look at one further illustration of how the AIDS epidemic has contributed to the conflict of physically healthy gay men. A young man had been in a relationship for several years, but during the third year of his relationship, which corresponded to about the third year of the AIDS epidemic, he began to develop increasing concern about the possibility that he had the disease. Neither he nor his lover, both of whom had regular checkups, showed any evidence of an impaired immune system. Nor was he significantly at risk from his past or current activities.

During the fourth year of intensive psychotherapy, Alan became increasingly concerned about a persistent lymph node in his neck. He had been assured that the node was probably related to drainage from a minor infection, but he was convinced that it was a manifestation of ARC (AIDS-Related Complex).

Alan's mother had been depressed during much of his childhood and he was burdened with feelings of guilt over her illness. He also experienced guilt over his feelings for his father and remorse at siding with his mother, who denigrated him. As he became increasingly aware of his anger toward his parents and at times toward me in the transference, his AIDS anxiety became, for a while, more severe. His fantasied death was an expression of guilt over his anger, a guilt that was made more intense by the increasing contentment and pleasure he was deriving from his relationship and from his work.

All the men discussed thus far fear that they might acquire or have already acquired the disease as a way of dealing with guilt and anxiety over their hostile impulses and fantasies. Their fear is a symptom of masochistic tendencies. Unrealistic anxiety about spreading the disease may also be used by some who have repressed sadistic fantasies. One man who had been in a relationship for approximately nine years, for example, had a periodic fantasy that he had the virus and would infect his lover. Rarely had there been any sexual activity outside the relationship, and even then the sex had been perfunctory and safe. He had had receptive anal sex on only two occasions before his relationship, which antedated the epidemic. His blood tests indicated a strong immune system.

This young man had incorporated and identified with aspects of his abusive father. He feared having a temper like his father's and he avoided behavior or confrontations that might cause him to lose control. In his relationship with his lover he enjoyed being the active partner in anal sex, but with the increasing publicity about AIDS, he began to lose interest in all anal sex. When he did occasionally attempt penetration, he lost his erection. When he attempted to use a prophylactic to protect his lover from the fantasied infection, he became unable to ejaculate. The fear of giving his lover AIDS was a neurotic manifestation of his conflict over his anger and his unconscious sadistic fantasies toward both his father and his lover.

Aids and Homophobia

We have seen that the unrealistic fear of AIDS may be one manifestation, in some gay men, of a masochistic personality trait and, in others, of repressed aggressive and sadistic impulses. AIDS anxiety is particularly prominent in healthy gay men who have conflict about their passive anal sexual desires, expressed or not. However, a neurotic AIDS anxiety is not confined to the gay community.

One heterosexual man, married only a short time, became increasingly fearful of contracting AIDS after his wife gave birth to their first child. He became frightened of having casual contact with gay men in subways and in swimming pools, afraid that he might acquire the disease this way and give it to the baby. He had become jealous of the baby's relationship with his wife, and the fear of the child's acquiring the disease appeared to be one way of disowning his own sadistic fantasies.

This man, like Seth, was terrified of what he experienced as "feminine" aspects of his character. After the birth of his child he developed fleeting fantasies of being anally penetrated. These vague passive feelings were, by and large, defensively evoked in him because of his fear of competition with and retaliation from a very successful and aggressive father. For him, anxiety about being "like a woman" was preferable to challenging his feared father. What he experienced as a feminine desire, however, made him wonder if he might be homosexual, increased his concern about coming in contact with gay men, and made him even more frightened of and contemptuous of gay men. He began to make increasingly frequent homophobic comments.

Another man, married for several years, also developed AIDS anxiety after the birth of his first child. This was expressed first as an irrational fear that his child would acquire the illness from some insignificant contact with gay men in the neighborhood. He had four siblings whom he had felt displaced by and enraged at because of the time, attention, and affection they took from his overworked and emotionally limited mother. The fear that his child would become infected had its origin in an intense rivalry with and fury at his siblings, and was a displacement of his rage at them. Gay men, whom he believed were responsible for spreading the disease, increasingly became objects of his contempt. They became, in effect, the agents of his fury.

It also became clear from my work with him that some of his anger at gay men and his irrational fear of contracting AIDS himself were, as in the previous patient, related to fears of the "feminine" aspects of his nature. It was not a coincidence that these fears became manifest in both men after the birth of a child. The nine months of pregnancy may evoke some envy of and identification with a wife's child-bearing and nurturing capacities. Anxiety about being like a woman and uncertainty about one's masculinity inevitably follow in our society. Both men also retreated defensively into passive homoerotic fantasies and questions about their own heterosexuality as protection from the threat they believed they posed to their fathers' hegemony. Their homophobia, never before experienced, was fleeting but intense.

These straight men illustrate some aspects of the intrapsychic and psychological forces that are partially responsible for the homophobia developing in our society as AIDS spreads to the heterosexual community. From the viewpoint of a social psychologist, the increasing incidence of verbalized homophobia and anti-gay violence is mainly caused by the scapegoating of a distinctive minority by a majority as a way of dealing with frustration and a sense of helplessness in the face of this epidemic. In addition, however, an irrational fear of AIDS and the prevalent homophobia appear to be ways anxiety is expressed by heterosexuals and homosexuals alike, who are both made increasingly anxious by the daily publicity given to the dangers of anal-receptive sex. The unconscious at times expresses identification with the mother as fantasies of performing fellatio or being the receptive partner in anal sex. For heterosexual men, who usually have little impulse to act homosexually, these fantasies serve to ward off competitive feelings and the fear of retaliation. These fantasies are usually distressing to them (see Chapter 7).[1] Some heterosexual men attempt to deal with this anxiety through counterphobic, macho behavior and homophobic attitudes, mistaking this feminine part of their character as homosexual.

One sees homophobia at its most intense in adolescents who may engage in gay-baiting and gay-bashing as a pastime. For this age group, homosexual fantasies may be particularly vivid because of the conflict evoked by their need to be dependent on their parents and a cultural expectation to separate from them at the same time. Many adolescents experience these needs and wishes for dependency as feminine. To escape from longings to be dependent once again on their mothers, many adolescents have a need to assert their masculinity. The hatred of gay men is an especially virulent manifestation of the adolescents' attempt to deny regressive dependent wishes by expressing their aggression, equated with being male.

Gay men may also repress passive sexual longings and fantasies that they perceive and label as "feminine," and some find these fantasies repugnant. It is one basis, as we have seen, for self-loathing and homophobia. I do not minimize either the great importance of internalized social prejudice or the vicissitudes of early development in the self-hatred of some gay men. But I believe that the hatred of what is viewed as "feminine" in men by all men is of great importance to understanding the pervasive homophobia in our society.

I use the term "homophobia" because it has come into common usage. I do so reluctantly since it signifies the phobic avoidance of homosexuals, rather than the aggression that the anxiety evokes.[2] Most important, the term is inaccurate, because this hatred of homosexuals appears to be secondary in our society to the fear and hatred of what is perceived as being "feminine" in other men and in oneself, and not, it seems to me, of homosexuality per se.

All homosexuals are perceived as "feminine" simply because they desire to have sex with and love other men, whether or not they are conventionally feminine or masculine in behavior or appearance. The more feminine or different from masculine a gay man appears, the more hostility he generally evokes, unless he can be "campy" enough to make himself appear absurd, thereby neutralizing the threat to straight men. Men are made more anxious than women by perceived femininity in other men, and men are generally more homophobic than women.

We would expect to and do find homophobia to be most prevalent in groups in which men are selected to participate because of their "masculine" qualities and where individuals must deny, repress, or suppress their feminine attributes in order to maintain the public and/or private image of the group and in order to continue to belong. The military establishment, the CIA and FBI, and professional athletic organizations are among such groups.[3]

Homophobia is also commonly found in groups in which a value is placed on the individual's "feminine" qualities, but where "being a man" is prized within the structure of the institution or as part of the public image of the institution. For some men in such groups—for example, the Catholic Church and organized psychoanalysis—this paradoxical situation may cause a particularly high degree of anxiety and conflict about their feminine qualities.

The members of both groups are in part selected because they are able to tolerate a high degree of passivity and accept authority. Within the organizational structure of both groups, however, great importance is placed on being "a man." In the case of the Church, women are excluded from the priesthood, and in the analytic community gay men are generally excluded from training simply because they are not heterosexual.[4]

All epidemics in history are seen to serve a moral purpose. They are regarded as signs of human transgression and of divine will. The victims of contagion—e.g., tuberculosis and leprosy—have at times been isolated and victimized. The sick in general have been treated as if their suffering was deserved.

Except for syphilis, AIDS is the only potentially fatal disease associated with sexual transmission. Although one-quarter of all AIDS victims in the United States are intravenous drug users and the rate of infection in this group is rising with tragic and alarming rapidity while the rate of new infection in homosexuals has plummeted, it is the homosexual community which has been attacked and gay men who have been vilified as causing and spreading the disease. "AIDS sparks an epidemic of violence against homosexuals," declares a headline in *Time* as I write these words.[5] In New York City, reported attacks on gays jumped from 176 in 1984 to 517 in 1987, obviously a small fraction of the actual total.

A letter from the American Family Association soliciting signatures for a petition read in part:

> Dear Family Member:
>   . . . If you want your family's health and security protected, these AIDS-carrying homosexuals must be quarantined immediately. . . . These disease-carrying deviants wander the streets unconcerned, possibly making you their next victims. What else can you expect from sex-crazed degenerates but selfishness?[6]

And from a physician's editorial in a medical journal in 1984:

> . . . We see homosexual men reaping not only expected consequences of sexual promiscuity, suffering even as promiscuous homosexuals the usual venereal diseases, but other unusual consequences as well. Perhaps, then, homosexuality is not "alternative" behavior at all, but as the ancient wisdom of the Bible states, most certainly pathologic.[7]

It is true that some gay men have flaunted the right to their sexuality, including the right to sexual excess, during the liberation years of the seventies and the beginning of the eighties. But the view that all gay men are or have been sexually promiscuous is a pernicious stereotype directed at one time or another against all minorities who are feared because of their difference.

It is now believed that it is not the number of sexual acts or partners but the nature of the sexual act that accounts for the transmission of this deadly virus. Why is promiscuity mentioned so often and why is anal-receptive sex, the sex act by which the virus is most easily transmitted, mentioned so rarely? Anal sex is the most graphic reminder of what is seen as man's playing a female role, and this sexual activity can barely be written about, much less discussed and described.

I believe there is an abiding primitive disgust associated with women in our society, and cultural evidence suggests that it is in societies in which femininity is seen as "pollution" that feminine character traits in males will be most feared.[8] Such negative traits as envy, jealousy, pettiness, seductiveness are all associated with women.

One irony of the AIDS crisis is that love, warmth, caring, nurturing, and nourishing, which are characteristics associated with women, have enabled gay men to prolong and save lives. AIDS has organized gay men and mobilized a community to become an effective agent for social and political change.

6

Lovers and Others: Gay Relationships

THE IMPRESSION that all gay men are promiscuous has been recently fueled by the AIDS crisis. The stereotype of homosexuals being constantly on the lookout for all sorts of sexual activity was first challenged by Kinsey and his associates, who found that predominantly homosexual men in fact had less frequent sexual contacts over a lifetime than heterosexuals.[1] It is also true that gay men have a high number of different sex partners throughout their lives, probably significantly higher than heterosexual men.[2] The number of different sex partners in a gay man's life does not preclude the same man's involvement in a loving relationship over an extended period, or his having times of sexual inactivity. The fact that gay men generally have less frequent sexual contact than heterosexuals suggests that solitary masturbation may be a preferred form of sexual activity for some gay men during certain periods of their lives.

There are three categories of gay relationships: long-term relationships, which I am defining as lasting one year or longer;

short-term, defined as being from two or more nights to one year; and the anonymous sexual encounter.

Anonymous sexual encounters generally occur in public rest rooms, gay movie houses, bookstores with booths, or parks and bathhouses. Such encounters serve different functions for different men at different times. For example, they may provide sexual diversity for some gay men in a relationship, who may use them to preserve the emotional fidelity and stability of the relationship. I will return to this point later.

They also provide a sexual outlet for closeted gay and bisexual men. In one study it was shown that the men most likely to engage in sex in rest rooms were those who feared disclosure or discovery because of their marriage or religious affiliation. In general these men are well integrated into a heterosexual community and appear to live conventional lives.[3] Usually, no emotional bonding occurs in these encounters, but considerable affection may be expressed.

Some closeted homosexuals find that the environment is as important to them as the sexual contact itself; they find relief and comfort just in being with other gay men. One man described feeling so safe and comfortable in a gay movie theater full of men like himself that he often fell into a relaxed sleep. Both in the surroundings and in the sexual contact there is respite from social stigmatization and debilitating prejudice and a temporary soothing of narcissistic injuries.

Some gay men who grow up feeling on the fringes of society because their sexual orientation is regarded with disapproval and censure may seek furtive sexual encounters in settings that are less than attractive or even grim. These settings are consonant with their feeling that they are "sexual outlaws." Rejection may occur there with varying frequency, but it is controllable, doesn't count for much, and causes little pain, unlike the rejection gay men experience from society.

Homosexuals, more frequently than heterosexuals, have brief sexual encounters in order to establish a social relationship. It is still difficult for many gay men to meet others socially, and though college campuses more often now provide organizations where this is possible, the gay bar and even baths before the AIDS epidemic have been traditional meeting places. For one gay man, the pornographic movie theater has been the only place he has met other gay men. He will have a sexual encounter, go to the other man's home or to his, and they will spend the night together. Through one such meeting, he had a relationship that lasted for several months.

Brief sexual encounters, both anonymous, recreational encounters and short-term relationships, cannot be considered apart from the social context in which they occur. There are no legal sanctions to bind gay men in relationships, as there are for heterosexuals: no marriage certificates, no tax advantages, and, usually, no children. Although we know that legitimization does not guarantee the monogamy of heterosexual couples or the stability of a relationship, the lack of validation has discouraged the formation and maintenance of gay relationships. Rage at social injustice has led many homosexuals to assert their right to have sexual relations that seemingly flaunt social convention.

Biological factors related to male sexuality probably play a significant role in the nature of the gay man's sexual activity and the number of partners he has during his lifetime. Human males in general are more promiscuous than females if they are left to their own devices and if there is the opportunity. "This is the history of his anthropoid ancestors, and this is the history of unrestrained males everywhere."[4] Males also appear to be less object-directed than women when it comes to gratifying their emotional and physical needs. Cross-culturally, women are less interested than men in variations of sexual partners.[5]

There are, in spite of all these developmental and social obstacles, many more long-lasting gay relationships than we generally acknowledge.[6] Until recently, there has not been much effort within the mental-health profession to understand the nature of such relationships.[7] Because of the hypothesis of pathological parenting and the concomitant conviction that all homosexuals are emotionally disturbed, there is a widespread belief that gay men are incapable of long-term relations.[8]

Some gay men, like some heterosexuals, do attempt to avoid intimate sexual or emotional attachments and gravitate toward short-term relations. Gay men may have particular difficulty with intimate relationships, which often evoke an unconscious recollection of the rejection and injury that they may have experienced during their childhood. The frequent rejection by fathers and peers in childhood and throughout adolescence contributes to a gay man's wariness of any relationship. By adulthood, confronted also with prejudice against the expression of their sexuality, many gay men are angry, hurt, and reluctant to risk the possibility of further rejection or to expose a partner to the rage which they perceive within themselves.

These developmental and social obstacles which cause some men to avoid intimate relations altogether may cause others to embark on relationships extremely guardedly in anticipation of rejection. Some harbor the unconscious intent of rejecting their partners, as they felt rejected as children, forming "spite and revenge" attachments. Such vindictive attachments do not characterize all gay relationships, of course, and in fact are not exclusive to gay relations, but they are frequent.[9]

Let us look now at some relationships of long standing as

they appear clinically, in order to understand some of the obstacles that gay men have to overcome to establish a viable relationship. David and his partner have been together for fifteen years. Each is concerned about the welfare and well-being of the other. They own their home together, rarely socialize apart, and share bank accounts. Although they love each other, David is constantly enraged at his lover, whom he feels frequently rejects and ignores him. During his therapy David discovered that, starting in childhood and continuing into the present, he had experienced similar feelings of rejection by his father and, to a lesser extent, by his mother. Far from being the helpless child, he can now retaliate by withdrawing or being condescending, which further infuriates his lover. Once he sees that Jonathan is enraged and is rejecting him in kind, he can rationalize his own anger and further withdraw. This cycle of fear of rejection, anger and retaliation, and further rejection is not unlike what one finds in many heterosexual relations; in many gay couples, the dynamics are typically related to remnants of anger from the father-son dyad of childhood.

Howard illustrates in a somewhat different way how this anger may be disruptive of an adult relationship. He and his lover have been together for five years. Howard is in his early thirties and his partner is six years younger. They live together, share financial resources, socialize together, and spend most of their free time with one another. Howard sought help initially because of work-related inhibitions and a general unhappiness and dissatisfaction with his life. While acknowledging his homosexuality, he had always had some conflict about it. His relationship with his lover seemed to be one area that was relatively conflict-free, but many months into the analysis it became clear that Howard was avoiding talking about aspects of this relationship that were troublesome and full of conflict.

Howard's father was emotionally abusive. He was very demanding of Howard throughout childhood and was rejecting and dismissive when Howard did not behave appropriately. His father had a vicious temper which he turned on him, the older brother, or the mother. So Howard found ways of avoiding his father's temper by becoming seclusive and secretive—"blending into the woodwork."

With his partner, Howard shows the same kind of withdrawal. Richard attempts to engage him in conversation and Howard responds in monosyllables and quickly seems distracted. He is sexually ungiving much of the time, and it takes considerable coaxing from Richard to get him to be responsive. This behavior provokes his lover to act like Howard's father; he becomes openly hostile and enraged. Howard describes these incidents as "expectable," stating this with a calm and assurance that suggest he takes a certain comfort in his familiarity with these feelings. Interestingly, he acknowledges that he selected his lover because of the man's seeming dissimilarity from Howard's father: he has a tranquil temperament. Richard's tranquillity and pacific nature, however, appear to produce a tension that comes both from being unfamiliar and from Howard's longing to be close to his father. It is both the tension of unfamiliarity and the longing for his father that cause him to provoke Richard.

Neither of these couples explicitly tolerates sex outside of the relationship, and, by and large, both are monogamous. Many gay couples do, however, build into their relations a spoken or implicit contract that permits sex outside the relationship. Open relationships do not signify instability or lack of attachment, love, or involvement, any more than a closed heterosexual or homosexual relationship necessarily indicates stability, attachment, love, and involvement.

Emotional fidelity is not necessarily compromised by sexual openness; in fact, outside sexual contact may be beneficial to some relations. Intimacy may arouse anxiety because of an unconscious fear of rejection. Or early erotic feelings for and attachment to the same-sex parent stirred by an adult relationship may need to be disavowed. For some men, anger associated with the rejection by and withdrawal of the father may be a powerful motive for outside sexual activity, which may be used to dissipate anger or to aggravate the lover, to cause him to behave like the familiar, rejecting parent. Often, outside sexual activity may actually provide stability for the relationship by relieving tensions deriving from it.

In view of the inherent obstacles to a lasting relationship between gay men, what makes gay relationships work as often and as well as they do? For one, partners of the same gender have a degree of compatibility and mutual understanding at the beginning of the relationship that is unusual in partners of opposite genders. There is an instant rapport based on being the same sex that may make the initial period of the relationship very exciting.[10] It is the initial excitement that in part makes it possible for two men to enter into a relationship with enthusiasm.

This similarity, however, may prove a burden over a long period of time. Human beings appear to need a sense of difference in order to maintain the tension of sexual excitement, as well as the sense of growing together.

Many gay men select a partner on the basis of their perception of socially acceptable opposite-gender relationships, often those of their parents. Believing that similarity will most likely produce compatibility, as in heterosexual relations, gay men seek out partners of similar age, interest, or vocation. My impression is that sexual and emotional interest simply wanes more rapidly in such relations because there is neither the tension that promotes sexual excitement nor room for emotional growth.

Many successful gay relationships are based on a difference in the partners—a difference in age, race, social status, or personality that provides the complementarity that allows for the tension of sexual desire and also the emotional space for the couple to grow in.[11] Complementation is not so important to heterosexual relationships, because of the gender difference. Naturally, difference per se does not necessarily mean two people complement each other, and even when they do, that does not necessarily insure success in the relationship. In general, however, distinctions between the partners in same-sex couples are an asset in their sexual relations. In heterosexual relationships, such dissimilarities often are a cause of disruption.

Joshua and Michael have been together for nine years. Michael was brought up in a wealthy Jewish family, had a college education, and went to graduate school. He is now a successful Wall Street executive. Joshua was brought up in a lower-middle-class family, is Protestant, left home when he was fifteen, and did not attend college. There is a twenty-year age difference between the two. Both report that they have "grown together" in the relationship and each has become more tolerant of the other's needs. Michael has become more understanding of the effects of the early financial deprivations that cause Joshua's acquisitiveness, and Joshua is increasingly tolerant of Michael's emotional needs which stem from his maternal deprivation when he was a child. They describe a continual renewal that occurs from their trying to meet each other's needs. Furthermore, they both describe a persistent sexual excitement that binds them together in the relationship.

That is not generally found in long-term relations between partners more similar in age and with similar interests. This couple also tends to be more monogamous than many gay couples.

Another factor that holds gay relationships together is the great emphasis placed on emotional fidelity. Because there are no legal, social, or religious ties, the importance of emotional fidelity, with less emphasis than in heterosexual relations on sexual fidelity, is paramount. In contrast to heterosexual marriages, there is probably more honesty and less hypocrisy in gay relations with regard to outside sexual activity.

I believe there is greater sexual flexibility and a greater capacity for changing roles in homosexual men in a gay relationship than in heterosexual men in a heterosexual relationship. It is generally held, however, that there is sexual stereotyping in gay relations.[12] But such stereotyping is, in my experience, uncommon among long-term gay couples where sex remains important.[13] Although, for heterosexuals and homosexuals alike, pleasurable sex usually involves a wide range and diversity of sexual fantasies, the flexibility of sexual roles is more limited in heterosexual couples because of anatomical differences, social convention, and procreative goals. The inability of some gay men to change sex roles from relative activity to passivity and vice versa is usually evidence of sexual inhibition.

One man of thirty-three, a patient of mine, has been in a relationship for five years and has continually been the inserter in sexual activity, with his partner in the passive role. My patient has great anxiety about being in the passive role in anal sex and must continually take the more active part in order to diminish his anxiety in the sex act. His anxiety is associated with feeling that he is like a woman, connected unconsciously with passive longings (see Chapter 3). To maintain the relationship, his partner has been compliant, although verbally he rebels at being continually in the passive role.

Along with greater flexibility in sexual roles in gay couples, there may also be greater flexibility in their psychological sexual attitudes with regard to dominance and submission than one generally finds in heterosexual couples, where conventional gender roles are usually more rigidly adhered to. In a heterosexual man in our society a dominant attitude is usually prevalent, and he is traditionally the inserter; the woman is usually more submissive, not only because of her anatomy but because of the social roles enacted in the sex act.

The passive recipient in anal sex often feels that he controls and manipulates his partner and may even feel that he is the dominant partner. Even more frequently, the "active" sexual partner in fellatio, the person who is doing the insertion, may experience himself as passive, while the more passive-seeming partner, the person doing the sucking, may feel that he controls the act by modulating his partner's sexual needs. This flexibility is probably less frequent in heterosexual couples because of social convention and anatomy. For most gay men, maintaining gender and other conventional behavior has become less important because of the stigma that goes with being part of a fringe group. Where sex is tinged with social censure, the mutual needs of the couple are more likely to guide, dictate, and provide form for the sex act than the convention that often structures heterosexual sex.

The AIDS epidemic has caused gay men to take stock of the value they place on being emotionally unencumbered. Belief in the right to have multiple sexual encounters has grown out of defiance of social prejudice and of the heterosexual norms by which gay men have been judged. I know of no statistics about long-term relations over the past nine years, but my impression is that the desire to enter a lasting relationship is now significantly greater than ever. However, social discrimination against gay men during the AIDS crisis has increased the conflict many men feel about their sexuality, and also has heightened their fear of being more visible—which, paradoxically, has made forming lasting attachments more difficult.

A couple should be defined by the emotional bonding that has occurred; it is not physical proximity that determines the nature of the relationship. David McWhirter and Andrew Mattison describe 156 gay couples in relationships that extend from one to thirty-seven years, many of whom, living as they do outside the social mainstream, do not live together and have had to improvise their relationships.[14] Many gay men sleep in one partner's home or the other's but live separately, though they consider themselves a couple and may have been together for a long time. Two men I know describe themselves as a couple, though they live in different cities. It is not uncommon for one partner in a gay couple to be in a heterosexual marriage.

Alan Bell and Martin Weinberg find that men in close-coupled relationships are less likely to regret being homosexual than others and much more rarely experience difficulties related to their sexual orientation.[15] My clinical experience and observation confirm these findings. The capacity to fall in love and to maintain a relationship over time requires a high degree of self-esteem, or "healthy narcissism." For gay and heterosexual men alike, it entails overcoming the injuries caused by inadequate mothering and nurturing. For many gay men, it helps as well to overcome the injuries to self-esteem that accrue from paternal rejection and from peer and social stigmatization. Only a man with a healthy self-esteem can feel capable of being loved and of loving. Those who experience too much rage as a result of any of these injuries are most likely to consider themselves incapable of love and to believe that their homosexuality is responsible for their inhibition.

The disadvantages that accrue to gay men in our society who are involved in a lasting relationship are outweighed by the emotional healing offered by a loving relationship. Mutual loving and caring over a long period of time are, of course, important for any human being. To a large extent, however, it is only through such mutually loving relationships that gay men can ameliorate the wounds of childhood and those caused by society. The rest is, at best, temporary comfort—in all likelihood, illusory and futile.

7

The Homoerotic Fantasy of Heterosexual Men and the Question of Bisexuality

IN OUR SOCIETY, "feminine" symbolizes passivity and submissiveness and "masculine" represents activity and dominance. The desire to be like a woman may act as a defense against the danger some men feel is inherent in their assertiveness and competitiveness. "Feminine" desires take the form of what heterosexual men in our society experience and label as homosexual fantasies. It is interesting that the expression of the wish to be like a woman takes the form of homosexual fantasies, for such fantasies convey the notion that gay men are by their nature passive and submissive.[1]

Defensive homosexuality is seen most frequently in heterosexual men who perceive their fathers as powerful, authoritarian, and frightening, and their mothers as submissive, dominated, and demeaned by their husbands. This view, which often has a basis in reality, is used by the heterosexual child to solidify his Oedipal wish to be his mother's ally and rescue her from the father. The perception that his father is demeaning his wife is fueled and enhanced by the child's competitiveness with and anger at him. It is a perception that adds to the child's unconscious fear that the father will seek revenge for his, the child's, competitiveness. Let us look at two illustrations of defensive homosexual fantasy from my analytic work.

Bob was twenty-three when he began his analysis. He had graduated from college with fair grades two years before, after excelling in high school in both academic studies and extracurricular activities. After college he went to graduate school but dropped out during the first year because he lost interest. He then worked in advertising but quit after six months because, again, he lost interest. When he started analysis, he was a salesman in a retail store. He sought treatment because he was concerned about his lack of motivation and his feeling of sexual inadequacy. He had a history of premature ejaculation and impotence with women, and was hardly dating at all because of anxiety about his sexual inadequacy. His masturbation fantasies were of erect penises, sometimes of performing fellatio, and, less frequently, of having violent heterosexual sex.

Bob's father was a wealthy, highly successful businessman. Bob perceived him as powerful, competitive, and emotionally detached, and, like himself, ashamed of tender feelings and contemptuous of tenderness in others. Bob recognized that he had been unusually close to his mother during childhood, and that she was inconsistent in her attitude toward his father— sometimes subservient but usually demeaning of him. Increasingly he became aware of his sadistic rage toward her and toward other women because of his frustrated early erotic longings and because of her attentions to a favored older brother.

By the end of the fourth year of analysis, Bob had success-fully completed law school and was working for a corporation. This period of success was in part motivated by a strong positive transference and by the fear that I would not like him if he displeased me. His achievements were accompanied by feel-ings of competitiveness with me, his father, and colleagues, and by homoerotic fantasies both in and outside of the analysis.

The night after he was complimented by his boss for an unusual and innovative solution to a complicated business problem, Bob had the following dream: "I was underneath some blankets with my shorts on. All of a sudden this guy was rubbing his leg against me. I wanted to get out from underneath the blankets but couldn't because my shorts were off and he'd see that I had a hard-on. He wanted to kiss me and I wanted to kiss him, too. I had this sexual feeling even though I was resisting it." His thoughts were of sexual feelings for me, of feeling small and powerless and helpless. He then remembered more of the dream: that his legs were spread like a woman's. He commented that his penis was small like a clitoris and that he felt helpless and unable to do anything by himself, just like a woman. He wondered what it would feel like to be anally penetrated by me.

As Bob's analysis progressed and he became more in touch with his previously unconscious competitiveness with his father and his rage at his mother, he began to have even greater success in work-related endeavors and he experienced more sexual pleasure with women. His anxiety then increased again, however, and he had more frequent homosexual fantasies of fondling either my penis or some other man's, of being anally penetrated, or of performing fellatio. He had no sexual en-counters with other men, nor had he ever had any homoerotic experiences. There was and never had been any strong incli-nation to do so.

On occasion during his analytic hours he called my attention to his erections in a casual, offhand, but playfully seductive manner, repeating exhibitionistic childhood sex play with his mother. Through his homoerotic fantasies and exhibitionistic behavior he was attempting to demonstrate both to himself and to me that he was no threat, that I would not attack him for his newfound vocational and sexual successes. Fantasizing and behaving in ways he believed were like a woman's, he attempted to neutralize this threat. During this time there was no interest in having sex with another man. Rather, Bob continued to have a pervasive heterosexual drive and increasingly satisfying heterosexual encounters. As the analysis progressed and drew to a termination, and his aggression and competitiveness became less of a conflict, Bob became more comfortable with his angry fantasies and less concerned about possible retaliation. His homoerotic fantasies gradually diminished and were largely replaced with heterosexual fantasies.

Another young man's history further illustrates how a heterosexual may have homosexual feelings, activated by aggression and competitiveness. Jack initially sought help because of a concern about premature ejaculation, his inability to feel close to women, and persistent fantasies of being forced to perform fellatio on men with large penises. He was also worried about his poor performance in graduate school and his inability to focus on any specific vocational goal. Like Bob, he perceived his father as powerful, authoritarian, and distant. He felt close to his mother but was furious at her for her devotion to his father, and spoke angrily of her being too easily dominated by him and of her conforming her life to his father's needs too much. He felt controlled by his father and believed that throughout his life he had been appreciated only if he did what his father wanted him to do. Jack's consistent inability to find gratifying work became a way of frustrating his father's perceived ambitions for him. It was also a spiteful retaliation for his father's efforts to control him and for what Jack perceived as his lack of attention during Jack's childhood and adolescence.

Jack's sexual inhibition was a symptom that expressed his wish both to hide his aggressive impulses toward his mother and other women and to frustrate them. This gave way more readily to analysis than his work inhibitions, which served to disguise and express the more powerful and pervasive rage at his father. During periods of increased sexual activity and improved sexual performance, Jack would comment on frequent and troublesome images of erect penises and thoughts of anal penetration. There was little or no impulse to engage in homosexual activity, and throughout the analysis his heterosexual impulses remained strong. His growing awareness, in the analysis, of his competitiveness and his murderous feelings toward his father caused his homosexual fantasies to decrease in intensity and frequency.

In both these young men homosexual fantasies were first activated in late adolescence by the threat the young men imagined they posed to their powerful fathers because of early academic success. Each was expressing through these fantasies the unconscious need to reassure his father by proclaiming: "Don't worry about my competing with you. I'm only a woman!" Inhibitions in sexual and vocational areas, along with homoerotic fantasies, served to diminish competitiveness and rage toward their fathers, whom they believed to be dangerous and capable of inflicting harm in retaliation. There was an additional advantage for both these men in perceiving themselves to be like women, since they believed they were pleasing their mothers by being more like them than like their fathers. In both, however, there was a strong drive for heterosexual attachment. In fact, heterosexual activity became enhanced during their therapy, without direction, reinforcement, or manipulation. Homosexual fantasies of being penetrated or performing fellatio were not motivated by a longing for other men but rather served to express fantasies of being penisless.

The following considerations may be helpful in distinguishing such heterosexual men—those who use homosexual fantasies defensively—from homosexual men.

1. Some adult heterosexual men may express the unconscious wish to be women, originating as a defense against conflict about assertiveness, through homosexual-like behavior and fantasy. The expression of "feminine" wishes opposes the dangers inherent in striving to be masculine, which is seen as being competitive and assertive. Some gay men may use homosexual fantasies defensively at times, but that is not the primary motive for the fantasy. There is evidence that the homosexuality of gay men, like the heterosexuality of heterosexuals, has a constitutional basis, while the form it takes is influenced by early development and early relationships (see Chapter 1).

2. In heterosexual men, homoerotic fantasies are usually first activated in late adolescence by the threats and dangers inherent in increasingly aggressive, "masculine" strivings. These fantasies are usually linked behaviorally to an inhibited sexuality and inhibited vocational endeavors as an attempt to neutralize these imagined dangers. In gay men, the homosexual fantasy is usually first present at a much earlier age, at about four. There is no link of the fantasies to inhibitions in sexual or vocational endeavors.

3. Homoerotic fantasy, when it occurs in a heterosexual man, is a defense against heterosexuality, which is perceived as threatening because of the anxiety associated with conventional masculine strivings. There is still a strong, though con-

flict-ridden, drive for heterosexuality, and there is little or no interest in attachment to another man. In the gay male, homosexual behavior and fantasy have as their aim attachment to another man, although, as with a heterosexual man's behavior with women, this is not the only aim, nor necessarily the conscious aim of the sexual fantasy or behavior. Hypersexuality and sexualization may be used by both homosexuals and heterosexuals to avoid such attachments.

4. Most, although certainly not all, heterosexuals enjoy conventional aggressive and competitive activities during childhood. Many homosexual men have a history of aversion to and avoidance of such activities in childhood.

5. Some heterosexual men have the feeling of having been different from their same-sex peers as children; nearly all gay men have a distinct recollection of an early sense of "difference." This sense of "difference" often acts as a screen memory; gay men recall being different rather than the conflict-ridden same-sex feelings and fantasies of their childhood (see Chapter 2).

6. In heterosexuals, by and large, the homoerotic fantasy feels unnatural. In homosexual men, this fantasy and behavior feel natural and normal. At some time in their lives, most gay men will feel that their homosexuality is socially disadvantageous and they might wish to be more conventional in their sexuality. Such a wish, based on a realistic appraisal and the fear of social bias and discrimination, must not be confused with or misinterpreted as an expression of underlying latent heterosexuality. For most gay men, heterosexual fantasies are experienced as being as alien as homosexual fantasies are to heterosexual men.

7. In heterosexual men, homosexual fantasies either disappear or become greatly mitigated in any therapy that is conducted in a neutral, unmanipulative, and uncoercive manner.

In the gay man, homosexual fantasies and behavior usually become less conflict-ridden during a properly conducted therapy, and both the strength of sexual desire and the potential for sexual intimacy with another man become enhanced.

8. In heterosexual men, the homoerotic fantasy is more likely to appear at times of conflict centering on aggression and competitiveness, both with a therapist and with others outside of treatment. In gay men, same-sex fantasies remain comparatively constant and strong, during a noncoercive therapy and outside of therapy as well. The degree of sexual desire and the nature of the homoerotic fantasy may, of course, vary during times of stress and conflict in a gay man's life. They also change at times of heightened transference and as a patient's homosexuality becomes less distorted and less inhibited by neurotic conflict.

It is important for the clinician to be able to use these criteria to distinguish between true homosexuality and the defensive homosexuality of some heterosexuals, since confusion between the two may result in harmful efforts to change homosexual behavior in gay men. I will say more about this in the next chapter.

Bisexuality

Freud believed that all persons have an inherited bisexual disposition, and he linked this bisexuality to the development of homosexuality.[2] Some analysts and therapists feel that bisexuals are sick heterosexuals who are using their homosexuality to ward off anxiety-provoking heterosexual impulses or that they are homosexuals who with proper treatment can become functioning heterosexuals. There are, indeed, men who appear to be bisexual who are clinically defending against one or the other aspect of their basic sexual orientation. But there are also men whose sexual fantasy life is comfortably divided between same-gender and opposite-gender fantasies and who can function with pleasure and gratification with persons of the same or of the opposite gender. Usually they have the experience of having fallen in love with both men and women, but, for social ease and compliance, most bisexuals wish to get married or are married. Bisexual men usually seek therapy because the homosexual component of their bisexuality is producing anxiety or presenting social difficulties.

The most important therapeutic task with these men is to make their homosexual impulses conscious and tolerable. Men with a strong bisexual orientation may, through a traditional and neutral psychotherapeutic process, be enabled, if they wish, to live a heterosexual life relatively undistracted by their homosexuality. Unlike gay men, they seem to be able to derive enough emotional gratification and sexual pleasure from relations with a woman so that their homoerotic longings do not need expression. The emotional and sexual adjustment of a heterosexual marriage that most bisexual men favor in this society will, however, be based on compromise and will involve some renunciation of the homoerotic component of the man's sexuality. Some bisexuals are in happy marriages in which the wife is supportive of and comfortable with the expression of her spouse's homosexuality in a relationship or in occasional affairs or in random sexual encounters. For many, this has been the preferred adaptation. This is less likely to be so during the AIDS crisis. Wives who are sexually active with their husbands are not likely to be as tolerant, and bisexual husbands are more likely to renounce the homosexual component of their sexuality. For a bisexual man who chooses an exclusively heterosexual life, however, success depends on his being conscious of and accepting of his homoerotic fantasies and impulses, which can then be used in the service of his heterosexuality and his productivity.

This point is illustrated by Gerald, a man in his early thirties who came for help because he was depressed by his lack of job effectiveness and, more important, by his social isolation. He lived by himself and was subject to feelings of loneliness and bouts of tearfulness. He had a child who lived in another city with its mother, a woman Gerald had had a relationship with but whom he had not married. He was still seeing the child and the mother of the child, to whom he felt a considerable emotional attachment.

Over the past ten years Gerald had several girlfriends, but the relationships dissolved because of his feelings of boredom and his decreasing sexual interest. During the same period he had episodic random sexual encounters with men, usually younger and straight-appearing, whom he "serviced." He usually met them in parks or public lavatories at night, or occasionally in the lavatories of the building in which he works.

Gerald feels his main source of emotional gratification and attachment is women, but he has for many years felt that his boredom has something to do with his bisexuality. He would like to get married but fears the rapid dissolution of any marriage because of his homoerotic interests, however transitory and uninvolving they might be. His fantasy life is more or less evenly divided between homoerotic and heterosexual fantasies, both of which are equally compelling and of a sadomasochistic nature where he is the dominated partner.

During the initial treatment he remarked that he had had bisexual impulses from early adolescence but that his proclivity for conventional socialization led him to have many girlfriends during adolescence and sexual intercourse when he was about eighteen. It was not until several years later that he had a first homosexual experience, and he has had homosexual encounters three or four times a year but no sexual activity at all for two to three years because of the fear of AIDS.

He was eager to understand the reasons for his difficulty in establishing a close relationship with a woman, while at the same time he was perfectly cognizant but unaccepting of the homoerotic side of his sexuality. Although he had fallen in love with a man several years before, he did not feel he needed affection and love in a relationship with a man as much as he did in his relationships with women.

His mother was described as being somewhat distant and preoccupied, as was his father. Gerald felt rather detached from both parents, particularly from his father. He believed his mother was the more emotionally vital of the two. He had envied his younger siblings, who seemed able to capture most of the attention of both parents. As therapy progressed, Gerald was able to resolve some of his repressed hostility toward his mother and father, coming to terms with feelings of unrequited love and of longing from childhood. His relationships with women improved somewhat and he was better able to attain a feeling of attachment to the women he was going out with. Because of his fear of AIDS, he avoided homosexual liaisons, although he had the impulse from time to time to have sexual contact with men. The frustration of these impulses offered him less difficulty as he came to accept his homosexuality as an essential aspect of his sexual drive.

The question will always be asked, in the case of a man like this, whether or not he used the homosexual impulses defensively to deal with his unconscious conflict with his father by placing himself in a position that he perceived as feminine or nonmasculine and uncompetitive. However, I did not observe in him those dynamics which I recognized in the two heterosexual men described earlier. Both his homosexual and his heterosexual fantasies remained relatively constant throughout the therapy and did not seem to be dependent on transference or on other aspects of his internal life for their expression. Interestingly, he initially perceived both his father and his mother as distant and preoccupied. This perception was a defense against his erotic feelings for both, feelings that had been frustrated by their attentiveness to his younger siblings. His emotional distance was an expression of his spiteful and enraged refusal to acknowledge any need of or attachment to either parent.

Men like Gerald, whose erotic fantasies are more or less evenly divided between homoerotic and heterosexual, and who feel a need for emotional and erotic attachment to both men and women, are, in my experience, relatively rare. Many men who appear to be bisexual and who are labeled as bisexual because they are married are in fact gay. Many more gay men are married than we commonly acknowledge. Martin Weinberg and Colin Williams, surveying a population of 2,437 homosexuals in the United States, the Netherlands, and Denmark, noted that 17 percent of the sample had been married at one time, which also corresponds to the findings of Marcel Saghir and Eli Robins.[3] Another study of 789 homosexual men found that 10 percent had been married, and 5 percent were still married. In about 60 percent of this sample of married gay men, the spouse was not aware at the time of the marriage of her husband's homosexuality. Similarly, figures cross-culturally indicate that approximately 15 percent of all homosexual men either have been or are currently married.[4]

It would be difficult to know from these statistics which of the men labeled in the studies as homosexual are, in fact, bisexual, since data with regard to fantasy life is much more difficult to come by than behavioral data. But my clinical and relatively small sample would suggest that the vast majority of men who are married who might be labeled bisexual or who label themselves bisexual are in fact gay.

Harold, for example, was forty when he came to see me. He had been married for seventeen years but had engaged in no sexual activity for fifteen years, since the birth of his child. He believed that he was bisexual because for two years he had functioned fairly well with his wife, but he had and continued to have only homoerotic fantasies. He masturbated to homosexual fantasies, mainly ones of mutual masturbation or of just getting physically close to a man. He was also aroused by attractive men he passed on the street. In spite of the persistent appeal of these fantasies, Harold had not had sex with another man since a year or two before his marriage. At that time he had found gay sex gratifying, and he fell in love on two or three occasions, but he would not permit himself to remain in these relationships or to get to know his partners better. Basically, he abhorred the idea that he might be homosexual.

This man's character structure permitted him little pleasure from vocational or sexual activities, except for masturbation. He had a mother who was extremely constricted emotionally and unable to provide Harold with a sense of his own worth. His father favored an older sibling and had never given Harold a sense of himself as a competent, worthwhile, lovable human being. It was basically his rage at both his parents and his guilt over this rage that made pleasure an unachievable goal and the inhibition of his pleasure a punishment for this unacceptable rage.

After many years of treatment, Harold's relationship with his wife improved greatly: he became less withdrawn, more loving, and felt more lovable. He also derived increasing pleasure from vocational accomplishments and from his child. His efforts to function sexually with pleasure were futile, however, in spite of the fact that he was seeing a sex therapist to improve this aspect of his life.

Though Harold came to accept the fact that he was homo-sexual, not bisexual, he preferred to stay married, to maintain his conventional life-style and present a social facade of being "perfect," in his fantasized, futile effort to please his parents. Somatic symptoms of migraine, high blood pressure, and pain-ful intestinal spasms, all related to internal conflict and spe-cifically to conflict regarding his sexuality, disappeared as he learned to accept himself as gay. But he continued to deny himself the emotional and physical pleasure of a gratifying gay relationship or of gratifying gay sexual experiences and was never able to tell his wife of his homoerotic inclinations.

There are many reasons why a gay man marries, but most often it is as a denial of his homosexuality.[5] Some men may believe that their homosexuality is a passing phase or that it is symptomatic of a psychological disturbance and can be "cured." Others may be unable to connect a lifetime of homo-sexual fantasy with being homosexual because they feel homo-sexuality is so reprehensible. Other gay men, aware of their sexuality, enter into marriage because of family or peer pressure and the value placed on marriage in our society.

Some, like Harold, marry because of genuine love and af-fection for the partner, even though there is no erotic attrac-tion. This may frequently be the case in our society, where, because of social prejudice, the lack of role models, the early trauma of peer rejection or of rejection by the father, many gay men suffer from an inhibition of their capacity to love other men.

I do not question that gay men can marry, that they can have happy marriages, or that marriage may be a worthwhile compromise for some gay men. The resolution of Harold's therapy, which for him was successful, was that he remained married and was reasonably happy, although he was sexually inhibited. It is important to recognize, however, that "for a homosexual to marry simply for the sake of conforming with the accepted structure of society or in the hope of curing his condition may result in disaster."[6]

8

Psychotherapy
with Gay Men

MY PERSPECTIVE on the therapy of gay men is based on two convictions. First, gay men can live, as homosexuals, well-adjusted and productive lives with gratifying and stable love relationships. This is an observation based on my clinical experience and on extensive personal observation.

Many readers will believe this to be a self-evident proposition. Most dynamically oriented therapists and psychoanalysts, however, contend that the same conflicts in the early lives of homosexual men that have caused their homosexuality have produced such severe personality problems that it is impossible for a gay man to establish stable relationships and live a reasonably happy life. These therapists believe that it is in the best interest of the homosexual patient to change his sexual orientation from homosexuality to heterosexuality. A homosexual man will then presumably be happier, not only because he will be in less conflict with society but because warring intrapsychic structures will have been brought into greater harmony through his understanding and resolution of his early conflicts. After successful treatment his homosexual impulses will theoretically have become successfully sublimated by a strengthened ego.

My second conviction is one established by clinical experience: the effort to change the sexual orientation of a gay man is harmful to him. The psychoanalytic literature is replete with recommendations for modifications of analytic technique that are deemed to be appropriate to the treatment of homosexual men in order to change their sexual object choice. For example, Lawrence Kolb and Adelaide Johnson state that analytic neutrality should at times be abandoned so that the homosexual patient not misconstrue neutrality as permission for him to act out homosexual behavior. They indicate that under some circumstances therapists should terminate treatment if homosexual behavior persists.[1] Lionel Ovesey suggests that a patient should be given an ultimatum if he is making insufficient effort to perform heterosexually. "There is only one way that the homosexual can overcome this phobia and learn to have heterosexual intercourse, and that way is in bed with a woman."[2] He and others maintain that only those therapists who are convinced that a homosexual can be changed to heterosexual should undertake the treatment of a homosexual patient.[3] Charles Socarides suggests that the gratification of a homosexual be spoiled by interpretation of the meaning of his "perverse acts," and that he be counseled how to engage in heterosexual sex.[4]

Freud was not sanguine about the possibility of changing a homosexual to a heterosexual or about its usefulness. In his "Letter" of April 9, 1935, to an American mother troubled by her son's homosexuality, he stated:

By asking me if I can help, you mean, I suppose, if I can abolish homosexuality and make normal heterosexuality take its place.

The answer is, in a general way, we cannot promise to achieve it. In a certain number of cases we succeed in developing the blighted germs of heterosexual tendencies which are present in every homosexual, in the majority of cases it is no more possible. . . .

What analysis can do for your son runs in a different line. If he is unhappy, torn by conflicts, inhibited in his social life, analysis may bring him harmony, peace of mind, full efficiency, whether he remains a homosexual or gets changed."[5]

In another publication he was less ambiguous about the possibility of change, stating: "In general, to undertake to convert a fully developed homosexual into a heterosexual does not offer much more prospect of success than the reverse, except that for good practical purposes the latter is never attempted."[6]

Through certain therapies, homosexual behavior can be curtailed for varying periods of time and heterosexual behavior can be manifest for varying periods of time in some gay men motivated to attempt heterosexuality. Claims of achieving behavioral change in a highly motivated population of male and female homosexual patients have in fact varied from about 20 percent to 50 percent, with a variety of therapeutic techniques.[7] Such techniques, however, rely on behavioral modification with positive and/or negative reinforcement or, in a supposedly "neutral" analytic therapy, on the exploitation of transference. All these treatments depend for their efficacy on making homosexuality appear less desirable than heterosexuality, or on "spoiling the gratification." Such treatment has the ultimate effect of undermining the self-esteem of the patient by making him feel that his sexual orientation is unacceptable to the therapist as long as he remains homosexual.

Kinsey and his co-workers for many years attempted to find patients who had been converted from homosexuality to heterosexuality during therapy, and were surprised that they could not find one whose sexual orientation had been changed. When they interviewed persons who claimed they had been homosexuals but were now functioning heterosexually, they found that all these men were simply suppressing homosexual behavior, that they still had an active homosexual fantasy life, and that they used homosexual fantasies to maintain potency when they attempted intercourse. One man proclaimed that, although he had once been actively homosexual, he had now "cut out all of that and don't even think of men—except when I masturbate."[8]

In a study of 106 gay men, Irving Bieber and his associates claimed that 19 percent of those who had been exclusively homosexual switched to heterosexuality as a result of psychoanalytic treatment.[9] Wardell Pomeroy, a co-author of the Kinsey Report, has maintained a standing offer to administer the Kinsey research questionnaires to any of the patients who were reportedly cured. Bieber acknowledged to Pomeroy that he had only one case that would qualify, but he was on such bad terms with the patient that he could not call on him.[10]

My clinical follow-up of many gay men treated by another therapist has demonstrated to me that there may be severe emotional and social consequences in the attempt to change from homosexuality to heterosexuality. I will illustrate this conclusion with three patients whom I saw in long-term psychoanalytically oriented psychotherapy ten to fifteen years after the completion of a prior analysis in which such a change was attempted. In the prior treatment, sexual behavior was temporarily modified. Each patient remained homosexual in his sexual orientation, however, as evidenced by the continuing predominance of homoerotic fantasy, which remained unchanged by the treatment. Each of these men now had the additional difficult social and personal complication of a family.

When Milton consulted me, he was forty-seven and the father of two adolescent girls. He had married in his late twenties, shortly after the completion of a five-year analysis. Before starting the analysis he had had an active homosexual life, including a relationship with a young man who, he told me, had been the only passion of his life. He had never enjoyed sex with women before his analysis and during the analysis "learned" to enjoy sex with them. Although sex with men was not specifically prohibited, the love affair was proscribed by the analyst and sex with women was prescribed. There had been no homosexual sex since the marriage. Milton sought therapeutic help from me because of persistent depression, no zest for living, low self-esteem, apathy in his work, and no sexual interest in his wife, with whom he had not had sexual relations since the birth of his last child fifteen years ago. His masturbatory and other sexual fantasies were exclusively homosexual. He longed for the love of his lost youth.

Milton was a devoted father and husband. His wife knew nothing of his past homosexual life. He had no regrets over the change in his sexual behavior, except that he felt something was missing in his life—he called it a "passion." Even though he was not actively homosexual, I considered him homosexual because he still had an active homosexual fantasy life and continued to long for the love of other men.

This man expressed a great deal of anger toward his prior analyst for "manipulating" him. He grieved at having given up the passion that he spoke of so often. During his three years of therapy with me, his depression gradually decreased as he became more tolerant of his homosexual impulses and was able to think of himself as gay. He never resumed his homosexual life, because he felt it would disrupt his marriage, and he sublimated many of his homosexual impulses into successful creative endeavors and into his love for his children and male friends.

Milton always believed that his previous analysis had been a success. He had a wife and children, from whom he gained enormous pleasure. He liked the conventionality, the relative lack of stress in his life, and his professional success. It became clear in our work, however, that the denial, repression, and unanalyzed acquiescence that had been necessary for him to achieve the renunciation of his homosexual behavior had affected his zest for life and interfered with professional accomplishment, and that his analyst's failure to analyze these transference manifestations and defenses in his first treatment was in part responsible for the depression that motivated him to seek further help.

The question of whether or not he would have been happier living an active homosexual life is unanswerable. But it would appear that the first analyst's "health" values made it impossible for either the patient or the analyst to explore this other option. It was clear to me from my work with this man that much of the depression that followed the termination of his previous analysis was caused by the exacerbation of his low self-esteem and poor self-image, which were reinforced by the negative way the therapist perceived and interpreted this patient's homosexuality. These symptoms were greatly alleviated in the subsequent therapy as he became more tolerant of his sexual feelings, encouraged by an accepting, neutral therapeutic stance.

Another patient, Larry, had previously been in analysis for five years, during which time he had married and then separated. According to his recollection, he had felt homosexual since early adolescence and had engaged in homosexual sex since that time. He entered treatment in his twenties because of several unhappy relationships with other men and because of depression and ambivalence about being gay. He met his wife during this analysis; she was the first woman he had ever had sex with. Although his sexual relationship was not "great," he perceived it as adequate and for a time he gave up all homosexual activity. Subsequently, however, his work seemed increasingly tedious and he became depressed, argumentative, and apathetic. He resumed having occasional surreptitious homosexual sex, and the relationship with his wife continued to deteriorate, until they eventually separated. He stopped his analysis at the time of his separation, ostensibly because he felt his analyst was unempathic and rigid. He sought consultation several years later, when he was thirty, because of continuing depression connected with his low self-esteem.

When I first saw Larry, he had no interest in women and not much interest in having sex with other men, although he readily acknowledged that he was gay. He wanted a stable relationship, which his previous analyst encouraged him to believe would be possible only in a conventional marriage. This analyst had made the same technical modifications as had Milton's: he had questioned homosexual behavior without actually prohibiting it, and encouraged dating and any heterosexual involvement. During three years of therapy with me, Larry mourned the loss of his wife and the probability that he would never have children, and he began to have an active sex life with other men and in fact entered into a relationship.

In both these cases the man's homoerotic behavior was inhibited by the previous analyst's reinforcing what he believed was the more acceptable heterosexual behavior and by his use of a probably unconscious, disapproving attitude that served negatively to reinforce the man's homosexual behavior. For instance, the previous analysts had stated that homosexual relations would probably be of short duration, reinforcing the notion that heterosexual relationships were intrinsically better and more stable. Furthermore, both analysts used whatever ambivalence their patients felt about their socially discordant sexuality and the pain caused by social rejection to reinforce the idea that homosexuality was a result of childhood conflict and to encourage their patients to change. Neither analyst appeared to recognize that his patient's willingness to acquiesce to attempting to change his sexuality was a manifestation, in the transference, of a childhood desire to please and be loved by the father. Instead, the need to be loved was used by the analysts to help these men suppress their homosexuality.

Another patient had had an earlier analyst who appeared to be noncoercive, nonjudgmental, and unmanipulative. There were no modifications in technique and no obvious violations of what is generally considered analytic neutrality. My understanding, however, formulated during the patient's subsequent long analysis with me, suggested that the therapist's social values had in fact significantly though subtly interfered with the patient's treatment; the analyst had not been able to help him come to terms with and accept his homosexuality.

Thomas started his first analysis when he was in his early twenties because of conflict concerning his homosexual fantasies and a persistent lack of interest in women. He'd had homosexual masturbation fantasies and daydreams since before adolescence. When he first entered treatment he had never engaged in homosexual sex, except for very occasional adolescent sex play that was clinically insignificant. Throughout this analysis, homosexual fantasies were interpreted as simply being a defense against assuming aggressive male roles, which included having heterosexual sex (see Chapter 7). The analyst would refer to Thomas's homosexual fantasies and impulses as his so-called homosexuality. This implicitly conveyed to Thomas that he was not really homosexual, that what appeared to him to be homosexuality and what he feared was homosexuality could be analyzed and would disappear. He continued to have exclusively homosexual fantasies, but he did attempt to have sex with women to please his analyst. Shortly after the termination of the analysis, and still under the influence of the transference, he married. Sexual interest in his wife rapidly waned, however, and after several years of marriage he began to have homosexual sex. When Thomas came to me in his late thirties, he was depressed, agitated, in despair, and confused. He was "wandering between two worlds" and thinking of suicide as the only way out of his situation.

When I began to treat Thomas, it was clear that his perception of his previous analyst as being simply rejecting, negligent, and uncaring was a repetition of earlier experiences with his father. Yet his perception of his former analyst's intolerance of his homosexuality seemed to be accurate. The analyst's inability to help Thomas discover and accept his homosexual identity contributed to Thomas's later depression and to the situation he found himself in, which he felt was hopeless.

During his therapy with me, Thomas decided to tell his wife of his homosexuality. Their mutual caring and understanding enabled them over a period of several years to establish a marriage that allowed both to have outside relationships. I recently saw Thomas, four years after terminating treatment. His unconventional marriage was still intact, and he had a lover whom he cared deeply about and whom he saw regularly in a monogamous and emotionally gratifying relationship.

In each patient, the transference wish to be loved had been used by an analyst to attempt to change the patient's sexual orientation. This, of course, made it impossible for any of these men to understand the conflicts which were expressed in the transference. For example, because he wanted to be a good sibling, the first patient had acquiesced to his analyst's need for him to be heterosexual. His brother had been the actively rebellious one, and Milton won his place by being acquiescent and agreeable. The second man came to his subsequent therapy with an enormous unanalyzed rage connected with early narcissistic wounds. By pleasing his analyst in attempting to become heterosexual, Larry had hoped to win a long-sought and elusive love. He had been a replacement for a sibling killed in the war, and as a child he had felt neither understood nor appreciated, perceiving that he was treated as if he were the dead older brother. He came to feel that, like his parents, the analyst had treated him as if he was someone other than himself—his "straight" brother. He felt a lack of empathy on the part of his analyst and believed that once again he was unappreciated. Thomas, the last patient, had been rebellious as a child out of a frustrated longing for love that he had never received from his father. His passivity and acquiescence in his first analysis expressed a deep longing for the love of both his parents. By pleasing his analyst in attempting to be heterosexual, he hoped to achieve this always elusive love.

Not only had the understanding and exploration of conflict been limited in each of the previous therapies by the use of the patient's transference wishes in order to attempt to change his sexuality, but subsequent analytic exploration was made even more difficult by the patient's marriage. In the cases of Milton and Thomas, the two men who stayed married, it was much more difficult for me to come to understand them and their conflicts because they had too much at stake to integrate and fully acknowledge their sexuality. I am not questioning whether marriage and children were worthwhile compromises for these gay men, or for any gay men, or whether gay men can be happily married. I am only pointing out that the subsequent therapy was made more difficult by their social situation and by such factors as the denial, repression, reaction formation, and readiness to acquiesce which led them into marriage and into staying married.

Two other cases of gay men who came for help after interrupting or completing a previous treatment illustrate the severity of depression that may be caused by therapists who are unable to convey appropriate positive regard for them as gay men.

I have mentioned Carl before. He had been referred for further treatment after he left another psychotherapist, an experienced analyst with a fine reputation. He complained about severe dysphoria, an inability to form any kind of satisfying, lasting relationship, about a lackluster college performance, and about the lack of goals in his life. He also complained about being gay. His parents wished he were straight. His mother badly wanted grandchildren, and he wanted to please her. He had had friendships with girls, and on one occasion he had had intercourse; but his sexual fantasies from age eight or nine had been almost exclusively about boys. He felt a complete lack of interest in girls, although he enjoyed their friendship. He wanted to be able to fall in love and to have a boyfriend because he felt so lonely, but whenever someone liked him he began to find the boy unattractive and lost interest.

His previous three-times-a-week analytically oriented psychotherapy came to a halt because Carl felt that his therapist disapproved of him. Although he was never told explicitly not to be homosexual, whenever he mentioned having cruised a bookstore or having had sex the therapist discouraged this behavior. Whenever he told of going out with another boy, his therapist wondered why he did not devote similar energy to a girl he had met and seemed to like. The therapist's interventions served only to increase his need for brief sexual encounters and he came to feel that they were motivated by the therapist's disapproval of his homosexuality. His feeling that his therapist condemned his behavior and did not like him were analyzed as projections. Carl felt increasingly depressed, defeated, and self-critical.

Some of my colleagues would argue that Carl's description of his previous therapeutic experience was distorted because of past or current transference. His narrative had a ring of truth and reality to it, however, and was not unlike the histories I have heard from many other gay men. I am ready, therefore, to discount the idea that the recollection of the past therapeutic experience of the many men I have treated is in the main the result of distortions of memory. It became clear that Carl's anxiety concerning erotic attachment to his father, his wish to please his mother, and his internalization of hostile social values had all produced a ready transference to which his previous therapist had responded, not by attempting to understand the conflicts underlying Carl's wish to be "straight," but by complying with this wish.

At some point in intensive psychotherapy, every gay man expresses unhappiness and dissatisfaction with his homosexuality. The socialization of every homosexual involves internalization of the social animosity he experiences. Carl's despair over being gay was an expression of this homophobia. In colluding with Carl's self-hatred, the earlier therapist became a further expression and extension of the incorporated values of a hostile and critical society. Carl correctly perceived that his therapist was biased, but his identification with this trusted person's prejudice further reinforced his negative self-image and encouraged further brief sexual encounters, which in turn made him even more self-hating and severely augmented his depression.

Another young man whom I have also mentioned earlier

differed from Carl in many ways, particularly in the severity of his masochism and the manner in which he used it to evoke disgust, rejection, and attack. Benjamin had felt homosexual since childhood and had actively engaged in homosexual sex since early adolescence. He had neither heterosexual experience nor sexual interest in women. When he saw me, he depicted his sexual encounters as sordid and spoke of his shame and disgust at being gay. On more than one occasion he confided that he believed he would be happier if he gave up his homosexuality. His previous therapist had conveyed to Benjamin that his unconscious homophobia and masochism were related to his being homosexual and would be alleviated if he understood why he was homosexual, and they would be eradicated when he became heterosexual. Although Benjamin was ambivalent about being gay, he felt his homosexuality was an integral part of him and that his sexual passion was his only meaningful link to others. The direction of his previous therapy made him feel even more desperate, disillusioned, lonely, depressed, and enraged.

Positive regard and affirmation must be provided by the therapist if there is to be an atmosphere in which the patient may safely project, witness, understand, and untangle the negative self-images he has acquired from childhood experiences and relationships. A therapist who does not accept his patient as gay will reinforce earlier images that are reflected in the patient's self-deprecatory, paranoid, masochistic, or sadistic attitudes which are now interfering with his capacity for more positive relationships and experiences.

This therapeutic stance, when applied to the treatment of homosexuals, has been called "gay positive" by some and "gay affirmative" by others.[11] The terms "gay positive" and "gay affirmative" are particularly useful to stress the fact that traditional therapeutic approaches are "gay negative." However, affirmation of the patient as a person is essential for the treatment of all patients, not just gay men. There are some issues that are particular to the therapy of gay men: for example, the injuries arising from the frequent occurrence of paternal rejection and from social discrimination and stigmatization; internalized homophobia; and the coming-out process. Therapists and analysts, in order to work effectively with homosexuals, must have some knowledge of these issues and their importance. But no technical deviation from the customary therapeutic alliance and positive regard are necessary or indicated in the psychotherapy of gay men.

I am emphasizing here the importance of the undeviatingly uncritical, accepting attitude in which the therapist's thoughtfulness, caring, and regard for the patient are essential.[12] However, I do not underestimate the value of questioning, of uncovering, and of the usual interpretive work of any analytic or dynamically oriented psychotherapy. Nor do I advocate an unquestioning acceptance of all the patient's views and values. Rather, I am attempting to demonstrate that an attitude of positive regard makes therapeutic work possible, because it enables these patients to express and analyze negative transference distortions from both the past and the present. It also has therapeutic value because it is through the interaction with the therapist that any patient should acquire a new, more positive, and more accepting image of himself.[13] The following case illustrates how such a change may occur in therapy conducted with appropriate regard for the patient and his sexuality.

Edward came to therapy because of a long-standing mild depression. He was twenty-four at the time, a recent university graduate, and was now in graduate school. He was particularly distressed by his unsatisfying relationships and what he experienced as an inability to feel attached to another man. His earliest recollections of sexual fantasies, as he related them early in the treatment, centered on older boys. He had little erotic interest in and no actual sexual experience with women. He had his first sexual experience when he was fifteen with a man ten years his senior. He always felt attracted to somewhat older men, with whom he could feel protected and submissive.

Edward had never had a mutually loving relationship and he longed for one. Although he was not interested in anonymous sexual encounters, he would have one-night or somewhat longer affairs which left him unsatisfied. He felt degraded by his need to feel humiliated and by his passive sexual wishes (see Chapter 4). He felt unattractive and undesirable in spite of frequent compliments on his good looks.

It became clear during his twice-weekly therapy that Edward's need to feel humiliated by and in his sexual behavior was related to his guilt at his own rage, which he habitually turned against himself. This rage was caused by many factors, including his father's turning from him because of his unusual sensitivity and seclusiveness as a child and his disinterest in aggressive sports. As he grew older, he interpreted this rejection as a sign of his father's contempt for him as a homosexual. Contributing to his humiliation, sense of rejection, and rage was his mother's turning away from him when she became depressed during periods of crisis when he was a child. During three years of therapy, Edward came to an understanding of the sources of his rage, thereby becoming more comfortable in acknowledging and expressing it in ways that were no longer self-punitive.

Most important, my acceptance of him as a gay man provided an atmosphere in which Edward, without fear of rejection, could project onto me and learn to recognize his own homophobic attitudes. As he confronted his self-hatred—including aspects that derived from conflict-ridden passive anal sexual desires—his self-assurance and sense of attractiveness increased. His relationships and the sex he had with other men became more gratifying as he freed himself from conflict about his sexuality and about getting close to other men, especially as these related to his ambivalent longing for his rejecting father. As Edward reexperienced his hatred of his father, his erotic longing for him, and his father's hatred, he could always return to what he knew was my unambivalent and unambiguous acceptance of him as a gay man.

Therapy terminated after five years. Edward had then been in two relationships in which he had felt loved and loving. Sex had become pleasurable and generally free of the old feelings of humiliation. Both of us now felt he was capable of achieving the intimacy he desired and needed.[14]

I have indicated (Chapter 4) how important coming out to oneself and to others is to the healthy development of gay adolescents and young adults. Any successful therapy with a gay man at some time deals with this issue of gay identity and how early conflicts and those imposed by the internalization of homophobic social attitudes may interfere with the establishment of a positive gay identity. Harold, discussed in the previous chapter, achieved only a guarded awareness and acceptance of his homosexuality. Yet, even this limited success contributed to his being less withdrawn and depressed, increased his sense of well-being, and alleviated his somatic symptoms. The following brief history of another man in therapy further illustrates that work with internalized social prejudice leads to the patient's gaining a healthier identity as a gay man and to symptom relief.[15]

Gregory came to see me when he was twenty-two (see Chapter 3). He was depressed and anxious; he said he wanted to marry but was unable to establish a relationship with a woman. A prior therapy, which he felt he had gained from, had not been successful in helping him achieve his goal of feeling "less homosexual." He believed he was gay, but he was reared in a Catholic family and believed homosexuality was sinful. Furthermore, he desperately wanted to be able to marry because of strong family ties and fears of rejection.

Although his sexual fantasy life had been almost exclusively homoerotic since late childhood, his sexual history included homosexual and some heterosexual encounters. He had never had a sustained homosexual relationship, but he had had affairs of several months' duration in college. He had had many one-night encounters since college, although his adolescence had been unremarkable with regard to homosexual encounters. He also dated a lot of women during this time, largely to please his mother. His relationships with women were less compelling, since he did not feel the same passion for them as he did for men.

In therapy Gregory discovered that he believed his homosexuality would lead to his being rejected by his parents, and that his own homophobia was a displacement from childhood feelings of having been rejected by both his parents because of their depression and self-involvement. Over several years he became increasingly accepting of his sexuality, gradually acknowledging it both to other gay men and to close heterosexual friends. His depression began to lift, and he fell in love and formed a solid, passionate relationship with another man. As this occurred, he became more productive at work, more outgoing, and felt better integrated within himself. He no longer felt a need to be heterosexual. When therapy terminated after five years, he had been living with his lover for two years.

There is little doubt that, without psychological intervention, the social pressures that this young man felt would have caused him to marry. While it is always difficult to predict the outcome of a marriage, there is every indication that his homosexuality would have led to frequent homosexual encounters and probably to relationships which would have been difficult for most marriages to survive.

The outcomes of therapy which I have described would be unlikely if the therapist held the traditional view that the only normal developmental end point is a heterosexual one. This theoretical position will necessarily lead those who hold it to an ambivalent or, at best, ambiguous perception of the sexuality of any gay man. It seems to me that it would be impossible for such a therapist or analyst, even if he practiced what he believed to be a "neutral" therapeutic technique, to be, in fact, neutral, because he is siding with incorporated negative social values to the exclusion of or at the expense of other intrapsychic forces—for example, the inherent homoerotic desire. Inevitably, the tone of his comments and the direction of his questions will subtly convey disapproval which will contribute to the negative self-image of the homosexual patient.

It is my suggestion to gay men currently seeking psychotherapy that if they are to unravel and untangle the internalized homophobia and other aspects of childhood development that may contribute to their low self-esteem, they must have a therapist who regards them as capable of gratifying and loving relationships as homosexual men. Guiding a therapeutic endeavor with any gay man must be the therapist's conviction that his patient's homosexuality is for him normal and natural. Such an attitude, it seems to me, can be convincingly sustained only by a therapist who holds the theoretical perspective that homosexuality is a normal developmental end point for some men.

Today, the therapists most inclined to feel this way will generally be homosexual themselves, although there is no guarantee that a gay therapist will not himself be encumbered by his own early conflicts and internalized homophobia. This is a vicious, self-perpetuating cycle. Some gay therapists receive inadequate therapy themselves, for the obvious reason that they may not have been treated by persons who had a regard for them as gay men. Thus, they may not learn to understand their own internalized homophobia and will be hindered in understanding this factor in the lives of their patients.

In emphasizing the problems that analysts and psychotherapists may have in treating gay patients and the care a patient should take in selecting a therapist, I am not implying that psychoanalysis or dynamically oriented psychotherapy cannot be helpful. On the contrary, I feel that both may be helpful to these patients in the same ways in which they are helpful to heterosexual men and for the same spectrum of problems and psychological disorders. Unfortunately, the degree to which psychoanalysis and analytically oriented therapy are value-ridden has made it impossible to measure the true potential of such treatment for gay men. The confusion of health ethics with moral values has biased data and interfered with the conception and comprehension of the many ways in which homosexuality, like heterosexuality, can be expressed, some of which are healthy and some not.

The essential clinical task for any psychotherapist is to help his patient be as free as possible of the conflicts that interfere with his capacity to live as gratifying and happy a life as it is within his grasp to live. With all patients, heterosexual and homosexual alike, a therapist must act to lessen the burden of the instinctual sacrifices that society imposes and to help the patient resolve the conflicts that interfere with what for him is the most gratifying expression of his sexuality.

9

Society and Gay Men

WESTERN CULTURE has firmly delimited masculine and feminine characteristics and roles. It places greater value on traditional male than on traditional female attributes. These value-laden dichotomous roles are rooted in the aggressively competitive nature of our social structure. Aggressive spirit and energy make good entrepreneurs, and society prizes these attributes more than loving, sensitivity, sentimentality, generosity, and caretaking, which are viewed as more feminine virtues. We prize individuality when it comes to the exercise of a man's aggressive spirit, but are inclined to despise it in the exercise of those aspects of his nature that are not perceived as conventionally masculine.

The roots of homophobia, as we have seen, lie in the hatred of what is perceived and labeled as feminine in men. In societies where women are subjugated, feared, or discriminated against because men feel contaminated or polluted by them, "feminine" character traits in males will be despised. "In contrast, if men value women, then it is not considered bad if a male displays some character traits more like those of a woman.

Androgyny is not suppressed, as it is in the hypermasculine societies, but valued."[1]

Boys who have artistic sensibilities and interests, who may not be competitive or aggressive, who are sensitive and solicitous of the needs of others, who like "pretty" clothes and objects, are likely to be perceived as being more feminine than other boys. They may be turned from by their fathers in favor of male siblings, and are likely to be labeled "sissies." A few who for any number of reasons do not become sufficiently socialized and masculinized during their adolescence may grow into adults who epitomize to themselves and others the role that has been ascribed to them. Most often, gay men despise in themselves, not their homosexuality per se, but what they have been taught as children to perceive as being different, and what has been labeled first by others and then by themselves as being "feminine."

Society continues to be very reluctant to ensure that the dichotomous compartmentalization of roles and the undervaluation of women have not been translated into infractions on the civil liberties and rights of women. Our society has been even more reluctant to change to one in which the same value is placed upon sensitivity, compassion, nurturing, and loving as on aggressivity, competition, and productivity. Such a basic change in our society might enable many boys who are different in these ways to grow up feeling more valued and valuable. It might enable heterosexual men to perceive that men who love other men may also be masculine.

I have stressed the important role, in the development of gay men, of the father to whom there is an unusual and powerful erotic attachment. I've attempted to show that a father's rejection of his homosexual son because of his atypicality or the father's own anxiety has harmful effects on the son's capacity to form loving relations in later life and on the nature

of these relationships. Suspiciousness, reluctance to form lasting relations because of a fear of rejection, and a tendency
toward attachments based on a need for revenge are some of
the possible ill effects of the early rejection of gay men by their
fathers.

If the fathers of homosexual boys were accepting and loving
toward them, these children would have a model for loving
and caring for other men, a model that has not been traditionally available in our society. Fathers who nurture the development of their homosexual sons, who affirm their worth
by giving of their time and attention, encouraging and sup-
porting their sons' interests, and who are not dismissive or
censorious will help their sons to be capable, as gay adults, of
loving, affectionate, and sexually responsive lasting relationships.

Mothers who denigrate the fathers of their sons are likely
to instill in these children deprecatory views of themselves and
other men. Although such mothers do not create the homosexuality of their sons, there is ample clinical evidence that
they can make it difficult for both homosexual and heterosexual children alike to prize the ways in which the sons are like
the fathers they love. This may have a particularly profound
effect on the homosexual child who has such a strong erotic
attachment to his father. Deprecation of the father has its most
pronounced effect in later life when, as an adult, a gay man
seeks partners with whom to share his life. It may cause him
to see all men, including himself, as he learned to see his
denigrated father, as worthy only of contempt.

The close-binding mother may not necessarily denigrate the
father, but a son may become very closely identified with the
narcissistic needs of his mother and grow up to have little sense
of himself or his desires, needs, and ambitions. "What happens," asks Alice Miller, "if the mother not only is unable to

take over the narcissistic functions for the child but also, as often happens, is herself in need of narcissistic supplies?"[2] Gay and heterosexual alike, the sons of such mothers become men whose ambitions are so closely identified with those of their mothers and whose lives are so inseparable from them that they feel worthless except when pleasing them. These men tend to lack an emotional center of their own. They are usually enraged, feel enslaved to their mothers, and often develop masochistic tendencies because of their inability to tolerate this rage. As adults, they are constantly in search of their true selves and, consumed by this search, have difficulty forming lasting relationships.

Kinsey and his colleagues, all well-trained observers, tried to guess, before asking any questions, which of their adult subjects would have homosexual behavior in their history. They were able to guess correctly only 15 percent of the time with their male and 5 percent with their female subjects.[3] It is largely impossible, given our present knowledge, to observe young male children and predict which are homosexual. Most are initially indistinguishable from their peers, except by the nature of their sexual fantasy life. Later, some will develop attributes of sensitivity and unaggressiveness that make them unlike many of their peers. A few will be "gender atypical" and overtly feminine.

If some of these children could be identified early enough, it might be possible to counsel parents and family so that rejection, injury to self-esteem, and negative self-images would be minimized or avoided altogether. Fathers of homosexual sons could, for example, be counseled not to withdraw but to nourish their sons' interests and to share common activities. When necessary and appropriate, mothers would be counseled to encourage these boys to spend more time with their fathers. If the child is made to feel that his same-sex object choice is a normal aspect of his development, he will grow up loving himself and others in spite of being "different" and in spite of the bigotry that surrounds him. He will expect that to be loved is the natural result of being a lovable and good person. These children, having learned to love and respect themselves as homosexuals, will have the self-esteem necessary to love and respect others. It is this nurturing assurance that begins in childhood with the love of the parents that forms the basis for a healthy self-esteem and for the assurance necessary to deal with social prejudice and injustice.

The Hetrick-Martin Institute in New York City was established to meet the needs of homosexual adolescents and their families. Its unusual approach shows early success in minimizing the harm done by the social, emotional, and cognitive isolation of homosexual adolescents and young adults. The center counsels and educates the parents and, if necessary, the adolescents themselves. It provides opportunities for the socialization of gay adolescents in an environment that is supportive and designed to counter negative images by providing appropriate role models and education. Similar programs throughout the country would assist gay adolescents who need help with developmental difficulties.[4] Without the benefit of early intervention, most gay men will continue to be affected by the debilitating social prejudice that shapes the attitudes of parents, peers, and loved ones.

Our laws currently contribute to making stable relations between men difficult, and encourage transient, random sexual associations that can be hidden. Some states refuse to recognize the rights of individuals to private, consensual sexual relations between adults. All states refuse to grant legal status to relationships between adult gay men and make it difficult for gay men in loving relationships to enhance these relationships by adopting children. Michel Foucault put it this way:

In Western Christian culture homosexuality was banished and therefore had to concentrate all its energy on the act of sex itself. Homosexuals were not allowed to elaborate a system of courtship because the cultural expression necessary for such an elaboration was denied them. The wink on the street, the split-second decision to get it on, the speed with which homosexual relations are consummated: all these are products of an interdiction.[5]

Our society does not desire to see gay men in stable, responsible, mutually gratifying relationships. Such relationships are still too threatening to the sense of masculinity of men in most segments of Western culture. When the time comes that such relationships are fostered between gay men, when homosexual men and women alike will no longer have to expend so much energy and time in hiding and disguising themselves and finding secret ways to express their love and sexuality, there will be a release of creative energy that will benefit all society.

It takes enormous effort for gay men to maintain their sense of dignity and self-worth in a society that remains inimical to them and their sexuality. It will take an even greater effort and conviction for our society to encourage the self-worth and emotional health and well-being of gay men by sanctioning loving relations of all kinds.

NOTES

Introduction

1. Sigmund Freud (1935), "Letter to an American Mother," reprinted in Ronald Bayer, *Homosexuality and American Psychiatry* (Princeton: Princeton University Press, 1987), p. 27.
2. Freud. Quoted in *Die Zeit*, Vienna, October 27, 1905, p. 5.

   Freud's libertarian convictions appear clear in this interview. Less well known is the fact that he signed a 1930 appeal to the German Reichstag to repeal that part of the German penal code that since 1871 had made homosexual relations a crime. This appeal is reprinted in translation by Herbert Spiers and Michael Lynch in "The Gay Rights Freud," *Body Politic* 33 (1977):8–18. The appeal was also signed by Arthur Schnitzler, Stefan Zweig, Franz Werfel, Jakob Wassermann, Dr. Hermann Eckel (president of the Austrian Bar Association), Professor Hermann Swoboda, and Professor Moritz Schlick. Their petition stated, in part:

   > Homosexuality has been present throughout history and among all peoples. . . . Their sexual orientation is just as inherent to them as is that of heterosexuals. The state has no valid interest in attempting to motivate heterosexual intercourse or marriage on the part of homosexuals, for this would perforce lead to unhappiness for their partners, and it is quite likely that homosexuality would reappear in one of the ensuing generations. . . . This law represents an extreme violation of human rights, because it denies homosexuals their very sexuality even though the interests of third parties are not encroached upon. . . . Homosexuals have the same civil duties to fulfill as everyone

else. In the name of justice, we demand that legislators give them the same civil rights by repealing the law in question.

3. Irving Bieber et al., *Homosexuality* (New York: Basic Books, 1962).
4. *The New York Times*, December 17, 1963, p. 33. The analyst Edmund Bergler also implied that he favored maintaining legal restraints against homosexuality, in the hope of encouraging a heterosexual adaptation (*Homosexuality: Disease or Way of Life?* [New York: Hill and Wang, 1957], p. 302):

> Up to now, homosexuality has been fought with well meaning and reasonable moral arguments and equally necessary legal restrictions. Neither method has been effective. Moral arguments are wasted on homosexuals, for when they flout the conventions they are satisfying their neurotic pseudoaggression. Threats of imprisonment are equally futile. The typical homosexual's megalomania allows him to think of himself as an exception. . . .

5. Anna Freud, "Acting Out," *International Journal of Psycho-Analysis* 49 (1968):165–70.
6. Sigmund Freud (1927), "Civilization and Its Discontents" (London: Hogarth Press, 1961) *Standard Edition* 21:59–145.
7. For an excellent critique of the psychoanalytic theory of male homosexuality, see Robert Friedman, "The Psychoanalytic Model of Male Homosexuality: A Historical and Theoretical Critique," *The Psychoanalytic Review* 73 (1986), 4:483–519.
8. Freud (1905), "Three Essays on the Theory of Sexuality," *Standard Edition* 7:141.
9. This letter was discovered by Dr. Hendrick Ruitenbeck and is in the Rare Books and Manuscript Library of Columbia University. It was first published in *Body Politic*, p. 8.
10. Russell Jacoby, *The Repression of Psychoanalysis* (New York: Basic Books, 1983), pp. 134–60.
11. Clarence P. Oberndorf, who was president of the American Psychoanalytic Association in 1923, wrote in 1953: "Psychoanalysis had finally become legitimate and respectable, perhaps paying the price in becoming sluggish and smug, hence attractive to an increasing number of minds which found security in conformity." (Quoted in Jacoby, op. cit., p. 155).
12. The first panel on homosexuality at a meeting of the American Psychoanalytic Association was held in December 1953 at the height of

the cold war and of McCarthy's investigations of homosexuals and communists in government. The proceedings of this meeting were titled "Perversion: Theoretical and Therapeutic Aspects" and were published in *The Journal of the American Psychoanalytic Association* 2 (1954): 336–45.

13. Other than in my own work, the main exception within traditional psychoanalysis to the conception that homosexuality results from a developmental disturbance is found in the recently translated work of Fritz Morgenthaler, *Homosexuality Heterosexuality Perversion* (Hillsdale, N.J.: Analytic Press, 1988). Also see Stanley Leavy, "Male Homosexuality Reconsidered," *International Journal of Psychoanalytic Psychotherapy* 11 (1985):155–74.

14. "Homosexual" is a medical term that originated in the nineteenth century. The Provençal word *gai* antedated "homosexual" probably by six centuries. See John Boswell, *Christianity, Social Tolerance and Homosexuality* (Chicago: University of Chicago Press, 1980), p. 43.

15. See Alan Bell and Martin Weinberg, *Homosexualities: A Study of Diversity Among Men and Women* (New York: Simon and Schuster, 1978), pp. 195–216.

Chapter 1

1. I have found this definition to be the most useful one for the assessment of sexual orientation, for organizing my observations, and for doing clinical work with gay men. It conveys my conviction that sexuality is an inherent, "essential" quality of all human beings. Some might feel that this definition does not take into account the different types of "homosexualities"; i.e., Bell and Weinberg, op. cit. Throughout this book I do attempt to convey that, like heterosexuality, homosexuality may be expressed in a variety of ways throughout one's life, and I describe the behavior of different gay men as it relates both to the exigencies of the men's development and to the impact of social prejudices. However, my clinical work and research from other sources suggest that homosexuality itself is present from earliest childhood.

Others might feel that my definition does not convey the complexity of sexual orientation; i.e., Eli Coleman, "Assessment of Sexual Orientation," *Journal of Homosexuality* 14 (1987), 1/2:9–24; and John De Cesso and Michael Shively, "From Sexual Identity to Sexual Relationships: A Contextual Shift," *Journal of Homosexuality* 9 (1983/84), 2/3:1–26. These authors are, I believe, elaborating dimensions of sexual identity rather than sexual orientation, and it is important to separate the two concepts.

2. Alfred Kinsey et al., *Sexual Behavior in the Human Male* (Philadelphia: W.B. Saunders Company, 1948).

3. Evelyn Hooker, "The Adjustment of the Male Overt Homosexual," *Journal of Projective Techniques* 21 (1957):18.

4. See the review by Bernard Riess, "Psychological Tests in Homosexuality," in Judd Marmor, *Homosexual Behavior* (New York: Basic Books, 1980), pp. 296–311.

5. Marmor, "Homosexuality and Sexual Orientation Disturbance," in Alfred Freedman, Harold Kaplan, and Benjamin Sadock, eds., *Comprehensive Textbook of Psychiatry/II* (Baltimore: Williams & Wilkins, 1975), p. 1511.

6. Clellan Ford and Frank Beach, *Patterns of Sexual Behavior* (New York: Harper and Brothers, 1951), p. 143.

7. Wolfenden Report (1957). Great Britain Committee on Homosexual Offenses and Prostitution. Authorized American Edition (New York: Stein and Day, 1963).

8. American Psychiatric Association, *DSM-III: Diagnostic and Statistical Manual of Mental Disorders*, 3rd ed. (Washington, D.C., 1980).

   The single remaining category of "ego-dystonic homosexuality," homosexuality that is "unwanted and a source of distress," was removed as a diagnostic entity from the recently revised *DSM–III-R*, 1987. For a discussion of the history of homosexuality in American psychiatry, see Bayer, op. cit.

9. See, for example, Sandor Rado, "An Adaptational View of Sexual Behavior," in Paul Hoch and Joseph Zubin, eds., *Development in Health and Disease* (New York: Grune & Stratton, 1949); Charles Socarides, *The Overt Homosexual* (New York: Grune & Stratton, 1968), and *Homosexuality* (New York: Jason Aronson, 1978).

10. Bieber, op. cit., pp. 85–117.

11. Freud mentioned a number of early environmental factors in the lives of homosexual men that might contribute to their "flight from women" to find love objects of the same sex. In "Some Neurotic Mechanisms in Jealousy, Paranoia and Homosexuality" (1922), he wrote of the child's fixation to his mother that impelled him to "look about for love objects

. . . whom he might then love as his mother loved him" (*Standard Edition* 18:230). At one time or another, he cited not only attachment to the mother but narcissism, fear of castration, a jealousy against older brothers, and the absence of a strong father as "accidental" or environmental determinants of the homosexual object choice. In a large number of cases of male homosexuality Freud felt that the identification with the mother was an essential determining factor ("Group Psychology and the Analysis of the Ego" [1921], *Standard Edition* 18:108):

> A young man has been unusually long and intensely fixated upon his mother in the sense of the Oedipus complex. But at last, after the end of puberty, the time comes for exchanging his mother for some other sexual object. Things take a sudden turn: the young man does not abandon his mother, but identifies himself with her; he transforms himself into her, and now looks about for objects which can replace his ego for him, and on which he can bestow such love and care as he has experienced from his mother.

But an emphasis on constitutional factors recurs in his writings. For example, as early as 1905, ("Three Essays on the Theory of Sexuality," *Standard Edition* 7:141):

> It may be questioned whether the various accidental influences would be sufficient to explain the acquisition of inversion without the co-operation of something in the subject himself. . . . The existence of this last factor is not to be denied.

And in 1923 ("The Ego and the Id," *Standard Edition* 19:33):

> It would appear, therefore, that in both sexes the relative strength of the masculine and feminine sexual dispositions is what determines whether the outcome of the Oedipus situation itself be an identification with the father, or with the mother. . . . It is this complicating element introduced by bisexuality that makes it so difficult to obtain a clear view of the facts in connection with the earliest object-choices and identifications.

12. Rado, "A Critical Examination of the Theory of Bisexuality," *Psychosomatic Medicine* 2 (1940):459–67.
13. Rado, "A Critical Examination of the Concept of Bisexuality," in Marmor, ed., *Sexual Inversion* (New York: Basic Books, 1965), p. 186.
14. For a review of the psychoanalytic views on the origin of homosexuality, see Bieber, op. cit., pp. 3–18; George Wiedeman, "Homosexuality, A Survey," *Journal of the American Psychoanalytic Association* 22 (1974)

3:651–96; Robert Friedman, op. cit.; and Bayer, op. cit., pp. 21–42

Some analysts have described all homosexuals as "psychopaths" because of the early injury sustained by their superego which may make it deficient or defective; i.e., Bergler, op. cit., p. 49; Panel (1954), op. cit. Other analysts have compared the ego of the homosexual to that of the schizophrenic; i.e., Panel (1954), p. 336, and Panel, "Theoretical and Clinical Aspects of Overt Male Homosexuality," *Journal of the American Psychoanalytic Association* 8 (1960)3:552–66; Robert Bak, "Object-Relationships in Schizophrenia and Perversion," *International Journal of Psycho-Analysis* 52 (1971):235–42. As one analyst recently stated: "We just do not find, except very rarely, male homosexuals without significant character pathology" (Otto Kernberg, "A Conceptual Model of Male Perversion," in Gerald Fogel, Frederick Lane, and Robert Liebert, eds., *The Psychology of Men: New Psychoanalytic Perspectives* [New York: Basic Books, 1986], p. 175).

15. Edward Wilson, *Sociobiology: The New Synthesis* (Cambridge: Harvard University Press, 1975), pp. 343–44. Also see Wilson, *On Human Nature* (Cambridge: Harvard University Press, 1978).

16. Wilson (1978), p. 143. Wilson defines altruism as "increasing the fitness of another at the expense of his own fitness" (1975, p. 117). Gay men who do not have children are able to care for relatives, such as nieces and nephews, both financially and in personal ways which theoretically assist them to have families and thus they are being "altruistic." By helping relatives, Wilson feels, homosexual men contribute more to subsequent generations than if they themselves had children.

17. For a critique of the sociobiological explanation of homosexuality, see Douglas Futuyma and Stephen Risch, "Sexual Orientation, Sociobiology and Evolution," *Journal of Homosexuality* 9 (1983/84), 2/3:157–68.

18. See Ralph Greenson, "Dis-identifying from Mother," *International Journal of Psycho-Analysis* 49 (1968):370–74; and Robert Stoller, "Boyhood Gender Aberrations: Treatment Issues," *Journal of the American Psychoanalytic Association* 26 (1978), 3:541–58.

19. Richard Green, *The "Sissy Boy Syndrome" and the Development of Homosexuality* (New Haven: Yale University Press, 1987).

20. See Bernard Zuger, "Early Effeminate Behavior in Boys," *Journal of Nervous and Mental Diseases* 172 (1984):90–97. Other studies indicate

the avoidance of "rough and tumble" activities in the childhood of homosexual men who were not patients; i.e., Marcel Saghir and Eli Robins, *Male and Female Homosexuality: A Comprehensive Investigation* (Baltimore: Williams and Wilkins, 1973), and also Richard Friedman and Lenore Stern, "Juvenile Aggressivity and Sissiness in Homosexual and Heterosexual Males," *Journal of the American Academy of Psychoanalysis,* 8 (1980):427–40.

21. Gunter Dörner et al., "A Neuroendocrine Predisposition for Homosexuality in Men," *Archives of Sexual Behavior* 4 (1975):1–8.

22. For a critical consideration of the biological model and its applicability to the understanding of sexual orientation, see Thomas Hoult, "Human Sexuality in Biological Perspective: Theoretical and Methodological Considerations," *Journal of Homosexuality* 9 (Winter 1983/Spring 1984):137–55. Also see Wendell Ricketts, "Biological Research on Homosexuality: Ansell's Cow or Occam's Razor?" *Journal of Homosexuality* 9 (Summer 1984), 4:65–93. For a general review of the psychobiological research, see Richard Friedman, *Male Homosexuality: A Contemporary Psychoanalytic Perspective* (New Haven: Yale University Press, 1988), Chapter 2. Dörner's research is evaluated by Louis Goren, "Biomedical Theories of Sexual Orientation: A Critical Examination," in David McWhirter, June Reinisch, and Stephanie Saunders, eds., *Homosexuality/Heterosexuality: Concepts of Sexual Orientation* (New York: Oxford University Press, in press).

23. Richard Friedman, op. cit., pp. 22–24.

24. There is no greater frequency of homosexuality in the children of gay and lesbian parents than in the children of heterosexual parents. See, for example, David McWhirter and Andrew Mattison, *The Male Couple* (Englewood Cliffs, N.J.: Prentice Hall, 1984). Also see Martha Kirkpatrick, Ron Roy, and Catherine Smith, "A New Look at Lesbian Mothers," *Human Behavior* 5 (1976):60–61, and "Lesbian Mothers and Their Children," *American Journal of Orthopsychiatry* 51 (1981):545–51.

25. Simon LeVay, "A Difference in Hypothalamic Structure Between Heterosexual and Homosexual Men. *Science* 253 (1991):1034–1037.

26. Franz Kallman, "A Comparative Twin Study on the Genetic Aspects of Male Homosexuality," *Journal of Nervous and Mental Diseases* 115 (1952):283.

27. J. Michael Bailey and Richard Pillard, "A Genetic Study of Male Sexual Orientation," *Archives of General Psychiatry* 48 (1991):1089–1096.

28. Dean H. Hamer et al., "A Linkage Between DNA Markers on the X Chromosome and Male Sexual Orientation," *Science* 261(1993):321–327.

29. Gary Mihalik, "Sexuality and Gender: An Evolutionary Perspective," *Psychiatric Annals* 18 (1988):40–42.

30. John Money and Viola Lewis, "Homosexual/Heterosexual Status in Boys at Puberty: Idiopathic Adolescent Gynecomastia and Congenital Virilizing Adrenocorticism Compared," *Psychoendocrinology* 7 (1982):339–46. Also see John Money, "Sin, Sickness, or Status?: Homosexual Gender Identity and Psychoendocrinology," *American Psychologist* 42 (April 1987), 4:384–99.

Chapter 2

1. A lack of conformity to conventional male behavior in "pre-homosexual" boys is described by Friedman and Stern, op. cit., and by Green, op. cit.

2. Green studied boys who were "feminine" and followed their progress into young adulthood. He describes a high incidence of adult homosexuality among those who were "gender atypical" in childhood. One cannot infer from these studies what proportion of gay men have gender disorders either in childhood or in adulthood. Two of my clinical sample of forty men had on two or three occasions dressed in some garment of their mother's when they were nine or ten years old. None of my adult patients had in childhood, from what I could reconstruct from their histories, a sense of being a girl and not a boy (a disorder of core gender identity) or had acted with any consistency like a girl (a gender role disturbance). For a discussion of the development of gender identity and role, see Phyllis Tyson, "A Developmental Line of Gender Identity, Gender Role, and Choice of Love Object," *Journal of the American Psychoanalytic Association* 30 (1982) 1:61–86.

My experience has been mostly with gay men who are successfully integrated into vocational settings, though many of them are to varying degrees "out" within those settings. It may be that my sample is not representative and these men have fewer gender disturbances than gay men in the general population. It is also probable that my data regarding childhood activity is distorted by every person's limited capacity to recall his childhood accurately.

3. Walter Williams, *The Spirit and the Flesh: Sexual Diversity in American Indian Culture* (Boston: Beacon Press, 1986), pp. 31–43.

Chapter 3

1. See Alan Bell, Martin Weinberg, and Sue Hammersmith, *Sexual Preference: Its Development in Men and Women* (Bloomington: Indiana University Press, 1981), pp. 61–62.

2. Bieber, op. cit., p. 311.

3. Also see Charles Silverstein, *Man to Man: Gay Couples in America* (New York: Quill, 1982), p. 25.

4. In his extensive interviews of gay men who were not in treatment, Charles Silverstein found that many had conscious sexual fantasies about their fathers. His findings suggest that many gay men have considerable access to these early erotic feelings. My sample may be biased, since gay men who seek help are often having difficulty in maintaining or forming relationships. It is possible that the unavailability of erotic fantasies about the father is more characteristic of this group than of gay men who do not have difficulties with relationships. I am inclined to believe, however, that repression of the erotic attachment to the father and of the sexual fantasies about the father are as normal as the heterosexual man's repression of his early erotic feelings for his mother.

5. I have found that castration anxiety or fear of injury from the father is more often the cause of identification with the mother in heterosexual men than in gay men, who identify with the mother to attract their fathers (see Chapter 7).

6. There is no evidence in my clinical experience that, when fears about receptive anal sex are experienced by gay men, they are related to the unconscious longing to be reunited in the mother-child dyad of infancy and to the anxiety that ensues from these longings; e.g., Robert Liebert in Gerald Fogel, Frederick Lane, Robert Liebert, eds., *The Psychology of Men*, p. 205. One would expect, if this is so, that anxiety about these fantasies and desires would be most intense in those gay men whose mothers were perceived as the most binding or engulfing, and this is not the case. Anxiety about such sexual activity, even before the AIDS epidemic made such fear realistic, may occur in gay men with every

variety of parenting. Also, gay men who have had a variety of mothering may have receptive anal sexual fantasies and may take pleasure in this type of sexual activity.

Chapter 4

1. What I refer to in this chapter as the process of consolidation and integration of sexual identity is conceptualized as part of the "coming out" process, by Vivienne Cass, "Homosexual Identity Formation: A Theoretical Model," *Journal of Homosexuality* 4 (1979):219–35; and by Eli Coleman, "Developmental Stages of the Coming-Out Process," *Journal of Homosexuality* 7 (1981/2):31–43. Consolidation may be roughly equated with coming out to oneself, and integration, with coming out to others. Rather than thinking of "coming out" as a goal in itself, I prefer to conceive of it as being part of the developmental task of establishing self-esteem.

2. See also Alan Malyon, "The Homosexual Adolescent: Developmental Issues and Social Bias," *Journal of Child Welfare* 60 (1981) 5:321–30; and Emery Hetrick and Damien Martin, "Developmental Issues and Their Resolution for Gay and Lesbian Adolescents," *Journal of Homosexuality* 14 (1987) 1/2:25–43.

3. James Baldwin, *Giovanni's Room* (New York: Dell, 1956), pp. 13–14.

4. Joel Hencken, "Conceptualizations of Homosexual Behavior Which Preclude Homosexual Self-Labeling," *Journal of Homosexuality* 9 (1984) 4:53–63.

5. Seymour Kleinberg, *Alienated Affections: Being Gay in America* (New York: St. Martin's Press, 1980), pp. 3–5.

6. Charles Socarides. Quoted in *The New York Times*, December 17, 1963, p. 33.

7. Panel, "The Psychoanalytic Treatment of Male Homosexuality," *Journal of the American Psychoanalytic Association* 25 (1977), 1:190.

8. Cass, op. cit.

9. Hetrick and Martin, op. cit.

10. Michael Ross, *The Married Homosexual Man* (London: Routledge & Kegan Paul, 1983), pp. 47–65.

11. Howard Brown, *Familiar Faces Hidden Lives: The Story of Homosexual Men in America Today* (New York: Harcourt Brace Jovanovich, 1976).

12. Ross, op. cit., pp. 1–37.

Chapter 5

1. One does not usually find competitive anxieties expressed as castration fears in gay men, but rather as free-floating anxiety or depression.
2. "Homophobia" was probably first used by George Weinberg (*Society and the Healthy Homosexual* [New York: St. Martin's Press, 1972]) to refer to the "dread of being in close quarters with homosexuals." The term was expanded later to refer to the hostile attitudes of societies toward homosexuals; e.g., Walter Hudson and Wendell Ricketts, "A Strategy for the Measurement of Homophobia," *Journal of Homosexuality* 5 (1980) 4:357–72. For a concise overview of this subject, see Marshall Forstein, "Homophobia," *Psychiatric Annals* 18 (1988)1:33–36.

One frequent rationalization for excluding gay men from these organizations is the necessity to maintain the morale or esprit of the group; it is believed that homosexual men would cause disruption and interfere with the organizations' cohesiveness. Many men fear that if they are in confined quarters and are denied the company of women, they will become homosexual. This fear becomes more intense in the company of gay men. It is true, of course, that there is situationally induced homosexuality, such as in prisons, but this behavior is occasional and transient, and heterosexual men return to heterosexuality when the confinement ends. Those who are gay will remain gay.

Even adolescents who engage in extensive homosexual activity over a prolonged period of time during initiation rites in certain New Guinea tribes return to heterosexual behavior after the initiation terminates. These are regarded as masculinizing rites of passage (Gilbert Herdt, *The Sambia: Ritual and Gender in New Guinea* [New York: Holt Rinehart & Winston, 1987]). I believe that it is clinically valuable to think of the homosexual fantasies and occasional behavior of preadolescents and adolescents in our culture as also serving a masculinizing function. For the fantasies and homosexual behavior are means by which the adolescent attempts to acquire strength from other men at a time when he feels under great social pressure to behave heterosexually.

The fervor with which most analysts promulgate the developmental theory that heterosexuality is the only normal end point and the clinical theory that only heterosexuality leads to a healthy and productive life may in fact be one way of expressing their anxiety about the passive, feminine aspects of character that have contributed to their choice of vocation and their being accepted for psychoanalytic training.

5. *Time*, March 7, 1988, p. 24.
6. Quoted in Dennis Altman, *AIDS in the Mind of America* (Garden City, N.Y.: Anchor Books, 1987), p. 67.
7. Ibid., p. 66. The editorial was by James Fletcher, "Homosexuality: Kick and Kickback," *Southern Medical Journal*, February 1984, p. 149.
8. Williams, op. cit., p. 268.

Chapter 6

1. Kinsey et al., op. cit. Also see Gordon Westwood, *A Minority: A Report on the Life of the Male Homosexual in Great Britain* (London: Longmans, Green, 1960).
2. See Bell and Weinberg, op. cit., pp. 81–93. Also Saghir and Robins, op. cit.
3. Laud Humphreys, *The Tearoom Trade: Impersonal Sex in Public Places* (Chicago: Aldine, 1970).
4. Kinsey et al., op. cit., p. 589.
5. Ford and Beach, op. cit., pp. 106–24.
6. Of the 686 male respondents in the San Francisco Bay area in the Bell and Weinberg study, more than a third were in couples. McWhirter and Mattison, op. cit., studied 156 male couples in relationships of one to thirty-seven years.
7. Silverstein, op. cit.; also McWhirter and Mattison, op. cit.
8. See, for example, Bieber, op. cit., p. 317:

> Some homosexuals tend to seek out a single relationship, hoping to gratify all emotional needs within a one-to-one exclusive relationship. Such twosomes are usually based on unrealistic expectations, often accompanied by inordinate demands; in most instances, these pairs are caught up in a turbulent, abrasive attachment. These liaisons are characterized by initial excitement which may include exultation and confidence in the discovery of a great love which soon alternates with anxiety, rage and depression as magical expectations are inevitably frustrated. Gratification of magical wishes is symbolically sought in homosexual activity which is intense in the early phase of a new "affair." These relationships are generally disrupted after a period of several months to a year or so . . .

Readers will recognize that this description can apply to heterosexual as well as homosexual relations. In falling in love there is an initial excitement, confidence, and unrealistic, even magical expectations. Prejudice about homosexual couples has blinded clinical investigators to such similarities between gay and straight relations; in others, the bias has obscured the distinct and intrinsic differences that may make a close and long-lasting gay relationship possible as well as unique.

9. As a therapist, I see many men who seek help because they desire to be in a relationship but are made too anxious by intimacy to enter into one. I see others who seek help in maintaining a relationship that is faltering because they feel inhibited or anxiety-ridden with their partners. I may hear more in my office about anxiety aroused by intimacy than actually exists in gay men on the whole. My casual observation of friends and acquaintances over many years, however, has convinced me that what I hear in my office is not atypical of gay men in this regard.

10. Clarence Tripp, *The Homosexual Matrix* (New York: McGraw Hill, 1975), p. 160.

11. Tripp, op. cit., pp. 57–59.

12. "Homosexuals typically use the husband-wife camouflage. . . . Every passive-feminine homosexual is paired with an active-masculine homosexual" (Bergler, op. cit., p. 20). Such statements illustrate the limitation of the perspective of a vast number of mental-health professionals who believe that gay relationships are analogues of heterosexual relationships.

13. McWhirter and Mattison, op. cit., p. 276.

14. McWhirter and Mattison, op. cit., pp. 9–11.

15. Bell and Weinberg, op. cit., p. 132.

Chapter 7

1. Defensive homosexual behavior and fantasy in heterosexuals has been called "pseudohomosexuality" by Lionel Ovesey. I agree with much of Ovesey's description of pseudohomosexual anxiety in heterosexual men. I do not agree with his view that the same anxiety motivates homosexual behavior in gay men as in heterosexuals (Ovesey, "Pseudohomosexuality and Homosexuality in Men: Psychodynamics as a Guide to Treatment," in Marmor [1965]), pp. 211–33.

2. Freud, "Three Essays on the Theory of Sexuality." (1905), *Standard Edition* 7:144–45.
3. Martin Weinberg and Colin Williams, *Male Homosexuals: Their Problems and Adaptations* (New York: Oxford University Press, 1974), and Saghir and Robins, op. cit.
4. Ross, op. cit., pp. 20–24.
5. Ibid., pp. 25–37.
6. Wolfenden Report (1957). Great Britain Committee on Homosexual Offenses and Prostitution. Authorized American Edition (New York: Stein and Day, 1963). Quoted in Ross, op. cit., p. 26.

Chapter 8

1. Lawrence Kolb and Adelaide Johnson, "Etiology and Therapy of Overt Homosexuality," *Psychoanalytic Quarterly* 24 (1955):506–16.
2. Ovesey, op. cit., p. 222.
3. "The analyst who undertakes the treatment of a homosexual must have already consciously or unconsciously arrived at certain diagnostic conclusions regarding the existence of an intrapsychic conflict . . . a conviction that a heterosexual solution is possible [and] that the patient will attempt it at some point. . . ." (Panel [1960], 3:566).

   Those therapists who favor a "flexible" analytic approach in which the patient is encouraged to behave heterosexually generally believe that homosexuality is caused by a phobic avoidance of women. See Bergler, op. cit.; Bieber, op. cit.; Ovesey, op. cit.; Socarides, (1968), (1978).
4. Socarides (1968), p. 222.
5. Freud (1935), p. 27.
6. Freud (1920), "The Psychogenesis of a Case of Homosexuality in a Woman," *Standard Edition* 18:151.
7. Marmor, "Clinical Aspects of Male Homosexuality," in Marmor, (1980), p. 277.
8. Personal communication from Alfred Kinsey to Clarence Tripp. Quoted in Tripp, op. cit., p. 252.
9. Bieber, op. cit., pp. 275–302.
10. This offer was mentioned to me by Wardell Pomeroy in a discussion in Bloomington, Indiana, in May 1986. The offer is also mentioned by Tripp, op. cit., p. 251.
11. John Gonsiorek, "The Use of Diagnostic Concepts in Working with

Gay and Lesbian Populations," *Journal of Homosexuality* 7 (1981/82),
2/3:9–20; Alan Malyon, "Psychotherapeutic Implications of Internalized
Homophobia in Gay Men," *Journal of Homosexuality* 7 (1981/82),
2/3:59–69; James Krajeski, "Psychotherapy with Gay Men and Lesbians:
A History of Controversy," in Terry Stein and Carol Cohen, eds.,
*Contemporary Perspectives on Psychotherapy with Lesbians and Gay
Men* (New York: Plenum, 1986), pp. 9–25; Cohen and Stein, "Re-
conceptualizing Individual Psychotherapy with Gay Men and Lesbians," ibid., pp. 27–54.

12. Within traditional psychoanalysis, the position of neutrality which I
have described is considered biased, because my goal is making a gay
man more comfortable with the "consequences" of his homosexuality.
That is, if the therapist does not regard homosexuality as pathological,
then his work is perceived as being biased by countertransference problems that favor the homosexuality and make proper treatment
impossible.

13. See Hans Loewald, "On the Therapeutic Action of Psychoanalysis,"
International Journal of Psycho-Analysis 41 (1960):16–33.

14. Detachment is frequently manifested in the transference during the
initial stages of analysis or therapy in the case of many gay men who
are frightened of and therefore defending against their longing for attachment and intimacy. We have discussed a number of reasons for
this anxiety, including, as in the case of Edward, repressed erotic longings for an ambivalently perceived father. It is essential to identify his
detachment in the transference to help a patient recognize how fears
of intimacy can keep a relationship from forming.

15. For additional discussion, see Malyon (1981/82), op. cit; Krajeski, op.
cit.; and Cohen and Stein, op. cit.

Chapter 9

1. Williams, op. cit., p. 268.
2. Alice Miller, *The Drama of the Gifted Child* (New York: Basic Books,
1981), p. 34.
3. See Tripp, op. cit., p. 99.
4. Hetrick and Martin, op. cit.
5. Michel Foucault, "Sexual Choice, Sexual Act: An Interview with Michel
Foucault," *Salmagundi* 58–59 (Fall 1982–Winter 1983): 10–24.

INDEX

academic success, 95–96, 98
acting out, use of term, 5
adaptation, social, 5, 102
adolescence, 47, 66, 85; AIDS epidemic and, 67; bisexuality in, 103; in case studies, 25, 27, 38, 48–50, 55–58; coming out to others in, 61–66; guilt in, 48, 56; heterosexuality in, 51, 56–57; homophobia in, 77–78; impediments to integration of positive sexual identity in, 57–60; loss of "feminine"-like qualities in, 19–20; masturbation in, 48, 53, 55–56; sexual consolidation in, 50–51, 54, 56, 66
aesthetic interests, 23, 25, 30, 34, 39–40
affection: anonymous sexual encounters and, 83; sex and, 35, 44, 47, 50, 52–53
aggression, 99, 100, 101, 116, 128; expression of, 64, 78; lack of, 18, 19, 28, 39, 70, 100; repression of, 75
"ah-ha" experience, 50–51
AIDS, 35, 67–81; anal sex and, 72–75, 77, 80–81; anxiety and, 68, 71, 72, 74–79; bisexuality and, 102, 104; in drug users, 79; education about, 72; fear of infecting children and, 75, 76; gay response to, 81; guilt and, 69, 74; homophobia and, 67, 68, 69, 73, 75–81; homosexual relationships and, 68–69, 73–75, 91–92; promiscuity and, 82; testing for, 67
altruism, 17, 140n
American Family Association, 80
American Indians, 30
American Psychiatric Association, 14
American Psychoanalytic Association, 136n–37n
anal sex, 44–46, 72–75, 96, 143n–44n; AIDS epidemic and, 72–75, 77, 80–81; fantasies of, 72–73, 75, 77; passivity and, 90–91
analyst-patient relationship, *see* patient-analyst relationship
androgen, 19
anger, *see* rage

151

anxiety, 7, 16, 24, 37, 43, 44, 143n; in adolescence, 48; AIDS epidemic and, 68, 71, 72, 74–79; of analysts, 37, 145n–46n; bisexuality and, 101, 102; castration, 143n, 145n; of fathers, 22, 34, 40; of heterosexuals, 76, 78, 95, 96, 99; intimacy and, 88, 147n; of married homosexuals, 54; passive role and, 90–91; in Rado's theory, 15

ARC (AIDS-Related Complex), 74

attachment, in homosexual relationships, 87–88

Baldwin, James, 51

bathhouses, 53, 83, 84

Beach, Frank, 13

behavioral modification, 111

Bell, Alan, 92

berdache, 30

Bergler, Edmund, 136n

Bieber, Irving, 4, 15, 112, 146n–47n

biological factors in homosexuality, 4, 6, 15, 17, 20–22, 99

biology, homosexual relations and, 84

bisexuality, 15, 18, 56, 101–8; AIDS epidemic and, 102, 104; anonymous sexual encounters and, 83; as defense, 101, 104; emotional gratification and, 102, 103, 104; marriage and, 102, 103, 105–6; in men vs. women, 16

body, attitude toward, 69, 70

boredom, bisexuality and, 103

Brown, Howard, 63

castration anxiety, 143n, 145n

Catholic Church, 79, 125

childhood, children: AIDS and, 75, 76; case studies of, 24–29, 35–42; early homosexual identity and, 23–31; homoerotic fantasies in, 23–24, 26, 28, 29–30, 35, 40, 53, 64, 99, 116; *see also* father-son relationship; mother-son relationship

choice, sexuality as, 16–17

civil rights, 67, 129

cold war, 7, 137n

coming out, 122, 144n; to family, 63–65; to heterosexuals, 63; to others, 61–66; as self-labeling, 48, 52–53, 55, 61; to wives, 65–66, 117

competition, 100, 101; father-son, 95, 96, 98; fear of, 75–76; mother-son, 42

conformity, 30; marriage and, 65

consolidation, sexual, 50–51, 54, 56, 66, 144n

counseling, parental and family, 131–32

couples, defined, 92

crime, homosexuality as, 13, 135n–36n

cultural differences, 30

"daddy's little girl," 43–44

dating, heterosexual, 49, 125

death, fantasy of, 74

decriminalization, 13, 135n–36n

defense mechanisms: homosexual fantasies as, 116; parent-child relationship and, 32–33, 37–39, 42, 54, 105; wish to be like women as, 99

denial, of homosexuality, 47–51, 107

dependence, homophobia and, 77–78

depression, 7, 16, 24, 35, 37, 43, 115, 125; in adolescence and young adulthood, 54, 55, 61; AIDS epidemic and, 69; analyst efforts to cure homosexuality and, 113, 114, 117, 120, 121; bisexuality and, 103; of mothers, 25, 74; overcoming, 54

Diagnostic and Statistic Manual of Mental Disorders, 14, 138n

disgust, sexual, 47, 48, 53, 58; overcoming, 49, 50–51

divorce, 54

domination, 57; by mothers, 14, 18, 21, 25, 32; submission vs., 91, 94; wish for, 28, 29

dreams, 35–36, 96

drug users, AIDS in, 79

education, AIDS, 72

effeminate behavior, 49, 53

"ego-dystonic homosexuality," 138n

ejaculation: inhibition of, 75; premature, 95, 97

emotional fidelity, 88, 90

environment: homosexuality and, 6, 14–15, 20, 138n–39n; for sexual encounters, 83

envy, 81, 104

epidemics: moral purpose of, 7–9; *see also* AIDS

erections, 97, 98

evolution, 17, 21

excitement, sexual, need for, 88, 89

exhibitionistic behavior, 97

family, 17; coming out to, 63–65; *see also* fathers; father-son relationship; marriage; mothers; mother-son relationship; siblings; wives

family studies, 20–22

fantasies: acting out, 5; AIDS epidemic and, 68–69, 71, 74; bisexuality and, 102–5; of death, 74; heterosexual, 100, 105; masturbation, 27, 53–56, 95, 106, 113, 116

fantasies, homoerotic, 11, 19, 27, 112, 116–17; in adolescence and young adulthood, 48, 50, 53–56, 70, 98, 99; anal sex in, 72–73, 75, 77; bisexuality and, 102–5; in childhood, 23–24, 26, 28, 29–30, 35, 40, 53, 64, 99, 116; fathers in, 28, 33, 143n; fellatio in, 77, 95, 96, 97, 99; of heterosexual men, 94–101; homoerotic behavior vs., 11, 12; in homosexuals vs. heterosexuals, 99–101; masturbation and, 27, 53–56, 106, 113, 116; passive, 44–45

fathers, 19; absent, 14, 32–35; abusive, 45–46, 64, 74, 87; anxiety of, 22, 34, 40; detached or distant, 14, 17–18, 22, 25, 32, 33–34, 38, 68, 70, 95, 104, 105; in homoerotic fantasies, 28, 33, 143n; hostile, 14, 34; identification with, 45, 74; longing for, 22, 26, 28, 87; mother's deprecation of, 130; rage of, 40; weak, 14

father-son relationship, 19, 25, 27, 32–47; adult erotic attachment and, 43–46; bisexuality and, 104, 105; childhood romance and, 35–39; competition in, 95, 96, 98; of heterosexuals, 75–77, 94–98; maternal interference in,

father-son relationship (*cont.*)
14; rage and, 68, 69, 71, 74,
87, 88, 98, 105, 106, 123–24;
repression of erotic desire in,
32–33, 37–39, 43–46, 70–71,
105; ways of attracting fathers in,
30, 143*n*; withdrawal in, 34,
39–41, 48, 70, 85, 88, 129–30,
131
fear: of AIDS, 69–81; of competition, 75–76; of exposure, 63; of
fathers, 95; of patients, 96; of
women, 14, 15
fellatio, 77, 91, 95, 96, 97, 99
femininity, 128; of gay men, 20,
22, 43–45, 70, 78; of heterosexuals, 75–76, 77; homophobia
and, 75–81, 128–29; of male
children and boys, 18, 19–20,
22, 24, 30–31; symbolic value
of, 94, 99
feminism, 16
fidelity: emotional, 88, 90; sexual,
84, 87, 90
flexibility: of psychological sexual
attitudes, 91; of sexual roles,
90–91
Ford, Clellan, 13
Foucault, Michel, 132–33
freedom, 54, 71
Freud, Sigmund, 3, 5–6, 14–15,
101, 110–11, 138*n*–39*n*; decriminalization of homosexuality ad-
vocated by, 135*n*–36*n*
Friedman, Richard, 19
friendships, between gay men and
women, 42–43

gay, use of term, 9, 137*n*
gay positive (gay affirmative), use
of term, 121–22

genes, for homosexuality, 17, 20–
21
Giovanni's Room (Baldwin), 51
Great Britain, homosexuality in,
13–14
Green, Richard, 18, 142*n*
guilt, 28, 48, 66, 74, 106, 123; in
adolescence and young adulthood, 48, 50, 56; AIDS epidemic and, 69, 74

harmony, intrapsychic, 8–9
health, use of term, 8–9
health values, acting out and, 5
hereditary factors, 17, 20–21
heterosexuality, heterosexuals: in
adolescence, 51, 56–57; AIDS
fears of, 75–80; anxiety of, 76,
78, 95, 96, 99; coming out to,
63; dominance and submission
in, 91; father-son relationship of,
75–77, 94–98; femininity of,
75–76, 77; homoerotic fantasy
and, 94–101; homosexual behavior of, 47–48, 56–57; homosexuality compared with, 4, 12,
17, 24, 29, 32–33, 48, 56–57,
82, 84, 86, 90, 91, 99–101,
115–16; in homosexuals, 7–8,
47–48, 49, 53–54, 56–57;
mother-son relationship and,
32–33, 94–95, 97; normal development and, 4
Hetrick-Martin Institute, 132
homoerotic fantasies, *see* fantasies,
homoerotic
homophobia: AIDS and, 67, 68,
69, 73, 75–81; fear of dependence needs and, 77–78; femininity and, 75–81, 128–29; first
use of term, 145*n*; homosexual,
58, 59–60, 73, 120–23, 125,

126; in men vs. women, 78; prevalence of, 78–79; of therapists, 109–10, 113, 115–20, 126–27; use of term, 78

omosexuality, homosexuals: abnormal, 4–5; causes of, 4–5, 6, 7, 14–22; closeted, 83; constitutional, 4, 6, 15, 17, 20–22, 99; as crime, 13, 135n–36n; cross-cultural statistics on, 105; defined, 11–22, 137n–38n; denial of, 47–51, 107; early identity of, 17–18, 23–31; "ego-dystonic," 138n; environment and, 6, 14–15, 20, 138n–39n; evolutionary basis of, 17, 21; Freud's views on, 3, 5–6, 110–11, 135n–36n, 138n–39n; heterosexual behavior in, 7–8, 47–48, 49, 53–54, 56–57; heterosexuality compared with, 4, 12, 17, 24, 29, 32–33, 48, 56–57, 82, 84, 86, 90, 91, 99–101, 115–16; in heterosexuals, 47–48, 56–57; homophobia of, 58, 59–60, 73, 120–23, 125, 126; homosexuals' resistance of, 7–8, 26–27; incidence of, 12–13; normal, 4, 8, 9, 12–13, 15, 17, 126; personal choice and, 16–17; prediction of, 131; relationships, *see* relationships, homosexual; use of term, 137; *see also specific topics*
homosocialization, 61–66; defined, 61; limitations on, 62–63
Hooker, Evelyn, 12
hormones, 18–19
hostility: of fathers, 14, 34; femininity in men and, 78; in homosexual relationships, 87; of mothers, 14, 60; of sons, 54, 104; *see also* rage

House of Lords, British, 13
humiliation, feelings of, 123, 124
hustlers, 35, 44, 59

identification: with fathers, 45, 74; with mothers, 18, 20, 25, 30, 44, 45, 58, 70, 77, 143
identity, sexual: adolescent development of, 48; AIDS epidemic and, 67–81; childhood and, 17–18, 23–31; positive, 8–9; positive, impediments to, 57–60
impotence, 44, 45, 54, 95
individuality, 128
inheritance, of homosexuality, 4–5
inhibition: of sexual behavior, 7–8, 11, 12, 69–72, 74, 90, 98, 99, 107, 108; work, 97–98
intimacy, 88; improved capacity for, 37, 38, 124; mother-son relationship and, 41–42; problems with, 16, 21, 22, 24, 26, 27, 40–41, 57, 64, 73, 85, 147n
intravenous drug users, 79
isolation, 30, 31, 61; bisexuality and, 103; epidemics and, 69–71, 79

jealousy, 75, 81
Johnson, Adelaide, 110
Jones, Ernest, 6
Judeo-Christian tradition, 13

kin selection, 17
Kinsey, Alfred, 12–13, 82, 111–12, 131
Kleinberg, Seymour, 52
Kolb, Lawrence, 110

lesbianism, as choice, 16
"Letter to an American Mother" (Freud), 3, 110–11

loneliness, 24, 27, 28, 38, 103, 121; in adolescence and young adulthood, 54, 61

longing for fathers, 22, 26, 28, 87

love, 9, 22, 56, 65, 71, 81; falling in, 49, 50, 59, 92, 102; in homosexual relationships, 87–88, 92–93, 124; parental, 132, 138*n*–39*n*; patient-analyst relationship and, 116, 117–18; self-esteem and, 55, 59, 92–93; sex separated from, 53, 106, 107

lovers, *see* relationships, homosexual

McCarthy era, 7, 137*n*

McWhirter, David, 92

Marmor, Judd, 14

marriage: anonymous sexual encounters and, 83; bisexuality and, 102, 103, 105–6; coming out in, 65–66; of homosexuals, 8, 62, 65–66, 83, 92, 105–8, 112–15, 117, 118–19, 125–26; of parents, 64, 70; *see also* wives

masculinity, 129, 145*n*; adolescent assertion of, 78; deficiency in, 14, 17–18, 25; symbolic value of, 94, 99

masochism, 16, 57, 69, 74, 121

masturbation, 82; in adolescence, 48, 53, 55–56; AIDS epidemic and, 68, 69; homoerotic fantasies and, 27, 53–56, 106, 113, 116

Mattison, Andrew, 92

medicine, psychoanalysis linked with, 6–7

Miller, Alice, 130–31

monogamy, 84, 87, 90, 117

mothers, 19; depression of, 25, 74; distant, 64, 104, 105; dominat-

ing, 14, 18, 21, 25, 32; hostile, 14, 60; identification with, 18, 20, 25, 30, 44, 45, 58, 70, 77, 143; rage of, 18, 21

mother-son relationship, 14–21, 25, 27, 38, 41–43, 55, 131; bisexuality and, 104, 105; disapproval and, 68; of heterosexuals, 32–33, 94–95, 97; love in, 138*n*–39*n*; narcissism and, 22, 35, 130–31; rage and, 57–60, 71, 74, 95, 97, 105, 106; rescue attempt in, 95; separation problems in, 16, 17–18, 58, 77–78; withdrawal and, 41

movie theaters, gay, 83, 84

narcissism, 16, 57, 62, 92; in mothers, 27, 35, 130–31

narcissistic injury, 57–58, 83, 92–93, 118

neuroendocrine factors, 18–19, 22

New York City, attacks on gays in, 80

New York Times, 4

normality, use of term, 8–9

Oberndorf, Clarence P., 136*n*

Oedipal stage, 14, 29, 94–95

Ovesey, Lionel, 15, 110, 147*n*

parents: coming out to, 64–65; counseling of, 131–32; marriage of, 64, 70; *see also* fathers; father-son relationship; mothers; mother-son relationship

passivity, sexual, 44–45, 72–73, 75, 90–91

pathology, homosexuality and, 3–9, 12–15, 33, 140*n*; AIDS epidemic and, 70–71, 73; Wolfenden Committee views on, 13–14 patient-analyst relationship, 27–29, 53–55; love and, 116, 117–18; rage and, 55, 71–72, 113, 121; transference in, *see* transference

Pearson, Drew, 63

peer relationships, 25, 47, 60, 66; in adolescence, 48, 55; rejection and, 28, 61; socialization and, 30

penis, *see* ejaculation; erections

personality disorders, homosexuality and, 4

Pillard, Richard, 20–21

Plato, 11, 22

politics, sexuality and, 16

Pomeroy, Wardell, 112

preadolescence, loss of "feminine"-like qualities in, 19–20

prejudice, 4–5, 6, 13, 16, 85, 132; adolescence and, 48; AIDS epidemic and, 69; gay defiance of, 91; respite from, 83; self-esteem and, 53; *see also* homophobia

projective tests, 12

promiscuity, 80, 82; in men vs. women, 84

"pseudohomosexuality," use of term, 147*n*

psychiatry, 6, 14

psychoanalysis, psychoanalytic theory, 3–10, 79; American, 6–7; education and, 72; legitimizing of, 6–7, 136*n*

psychoanalytic training, suitability of homosexuals for, 6, 7

psychotherapy: analyst's homophobia and, 109–10, 113, 115–20, 126–27; analytic neutrality and, 5, 110, 114, 116, 126, 149*n*; author's perspective on, 109; conflict-oriented view of, 109–10, 116; "curing" emphasis of,

109–21; gay men and, 5–8, 15, 53–54, 109–27; gay positive (gay affirmative), 121–22; gay therapists and, 127; proper application of, 8

Rado, Sandor, 15

rage, 62, 92; AIDS epidemic and, 71; of fathers, 40; father-son relationship and, 68, 69, 71, 74, 87, 88, 98, 105, 106, 123–24; in homosexual relationships, 21–22, 34, 85, 86, 87; of mothers, 18, 21; mother-son relationship and, 57–60, 71, 74, 95, 97, 105, 106; patient-analyst relationship and, 55, 71–72, 113, 121; toward siblings, 41; at social injustice, 84

rejection: in homosexual relationships, 85, 86; parental, 34, 39–41, 48, 70, 85, 88, 123–24, 125, 129–30, 131; peer relationships and, 28, 61; in sexual encounters, 83

relationships: father-son, *see* father-son relationship; mother-son, *see* mother-son relationship; patient-analyst, *see* patient-analyst relationship; peer, *see* peer relationships

relationships, homosexual, 82–93; in adolescence and young adulthood, 48–53; AIDS and, 68–69, 73–75, 91–92; anonymous, 54, 59, 83–85; biological factors in, 84; complementation in, 89; emotional fidelity and, 88, 90; factors in favor of, 88–91; flexibility and role changes in, 90–91; lack of legal sanctions in, 84; long-term, 82–83, 85–93; ob-

relationships, homosexual (*cont.*)
    stacles to, 84–88, 92; open, 87–
    88; partner selection in, 87, 88–
    89; rage in, 21–22, 34, 85, 86,
    87; rapport in, 88; short-term,
    83–85; similarity vs. difference
    in, 88–90; "spite and revenge"
    attachments, 85; withdrawal in,
    86, 87
religion, 50, 79, 83, 125
repression, 50, 65; of aggression,
    75; of erotic desire in father-son
    relationship, 32–33, 37–39,
    43–46, 70–71, 105
respect, 9
restrooms, *see* urinals, public
rivalry, *see* competition
Robins, Eli, 105
role changes, in homosexual vs.
    heterosexual relationships, 90
role models, homosexual: lack of,
    107; positive, 62, 130
roles, male, cultural differences in,
    30

sadism, 73, 74, 75, 121
Saghir, Marcel, 105
secretiveness, 30, 31, 53, 87
self-esteem, 9, 60; AIDS epidemic
    and, 68, 73; coming out and,
    144*n*; love and, 55, 59, 92–93;
    low, 26, 28, 54, 59, 65, 113,
    114, 115, 126, 131; social ac-
    ceptance and, 62, 63; under-
    mining of, 7, 16, 21, 27, 34,
    40–41, 47, 53, 92
self-hatred, 58, 59–60
self-image: poor, 16, 57, 114, 120,
    131; positive, 9, 51
self-isolation, 30, 31
self-labeling, 48, 52–53, 55, 61
sensitivity, 23, 24, 34

separation, marital, 114, 115
separation problems, 16, 17–18,
    58, 60, 66; homophobia and,
    77–78
sex, sexual behavior: abstinence,
    69; affection separated from, 35,
    44, 47, 50, 52–53; anal, *see*
    anal sex; experimentation, 68,
    71; fellatio, 77, 91, 95, 96, 97,
    99; fidelity and, 84, 87, 90; in-
    hibition of, 7–8, 11, 12, 69–72,
    74, 90, 98, 99, 107, 108; law
    and, 132; love separated from,
    53, 106, 107; passivity and, 90–
    91; of women vs. men, 84–85
sexual identity, *see* identity, sexual
shamans, 30
siblings, 117–18; coming out to,
    65; parental favoring of, 40, 41,
    70, 95, 104, 106
Silverstein, Charles, 143*n*
sin, homosexuality as, 50, 51, 68,
    125
Socarides, Charles, 4, 15, 110
social adaptation, 5, 102
socialization, coming out to others
    and, 61–66
society, gay men and, 5, 17, 128–
    33
sociobiological view of homosex-
    uality, 17
sons, *see* father-son relationship
"spite and revenge" attachments,
    85
status, 17
stereotypes: effeminate behavior,
    49; femininity, 20; promiscuity,
    80, 82; sexual roles, 90
sublimation, 113–14
submission, 91, 94, 97, 123
suffering, 68
Symposium (Plato), 11, 22

teachers, homosexual, 55–56
therapist-patient relationship, *see* patient-analyst relationship
Time, 80
transference, 8, 74, 96, 101, 105, 120, 149n; negative, 72, 122; wish to be loved and, 116, 117–18
twins, homosexuality in, 20, 21

urinals, public: as courting grounds, 53, 83, 103; as initiation sites, 52

Weinberg, George, 145n
Weinberg, Martin, 92, 105
Weinrich, James, 21
Williams, Colin, 105
Wilson, Edward O., 17, 140n
wives: coming out to, 65–66, 117; lack of interest in sex with, 113

Wolfenden Committee, 13–14
women: disgust associated with, 81; fear of, 14, 15; friendships with, 42; homophobia of, 78; lesbian, 16; rivalry with, 42; sexual behavior of, 84–85, 91; submission of, 91, 94, 97; undervaluation of, 128–29; wish to be like, 94, 96, 97, 99; *see also* mothers; wives
work inhibitions, 97–98
World War II, 6–7

young adulthood: AIDS epidemic and, 67–75; bisexuality in, 103–4; case studies of, 49–50, 53–55, 58–60, 68–71; coming out to others in, 61–66; of gay men, 47–66; sexual identity in, 57–60

Zeit, Die, 3–4